Coaching Basketball's Zone Offenses

COACHING BASKETBALL'S
ZONE OFFENSES

Delmer W. Harris

Parker Publishing Company, Inc.
West Nyack, N. Y.

Library of Congress Cataloging in Publication Data

Harris, Delmer.
  Coaching basketball's zone offenses.

  Includes index.
  1. Basketball--Offense. 2. Basketball coaching.
I. Title.
GV889.H36   796.32'32   75-29427
ISBN 0-13-139030-9

To: Basketball in Puerto Rica,
especially Hector Reyes,
Roberto Munoz-Zayas and
los campeons en todo, Bayamou.

Other Books by the Author:

Multiple Defenses for Winning Basketball

How This Book Will Help You Catch up with the Zone Defenses

A question debated frequently among basketball coaches is: which aspect of the game is more dominating at this moment, the defense or the offense? Over the years there has been a pendulum-like movement in answer to this question. Each time the offense establishes itself as dominant over the defense, along comes a technique like the switching man-to-man, a zone, a press, a matchup, or whatever panacea the basketball minds can devise to counter against the prevailing forces.

While it is a bit academic to debate which aspect is dominant at any given period of time across the nation or world, it is important for each coach or player to know his own strong and weak points. It is my opinion that through all the changes in the game, one area of the game has been lagging behind the others in theory. That has been zone offense.

In this book, I am attempting to close the gap between zone defense and zone offense. Over many years of coaching the zone defenses and offenses, I have seen a lot of moves that have helped me form a core group of moves which I call the Basic Five. By teaching these five fundamental zone offense moves, a coach can develop a system of play that we call Organized Free-Lance. It is a two-pronged attack in that the players may use any of the five moves in random sequence as openings occur in the defense which allow one or more of the five options to be used. Or the five moves may be arranged in any of dozens of specific sequences so that the team has a number of plays from

9

which to choose. The blessing is that once the five basic moves are learned, the team can go into almost any zone play or offense known and will be able to execute the specific parts because they have practiced the fundamentals of the Basic Five.

The starting point for any team is to realize that the zones are not only different from the man-to-man, but that they differ from each other, as well. When players learn to see when a team begins to match up or to get out into the lanes, they can then make better responses to the defense. Second, the team must be steeped in some practical theory and philosophy as to how a team can make zone defenses suffer in general. In the book I demonstrate how you can develop your game to beat the zones even when you cannot shoot over the top of the zones. There are specific theories of penetration through the use of cutting and dribble-moves that give the team with little outside shooting a reason to expect to be able to go successfully against the zones anyway.

After recognition of the defense and knowing how to attack zones in theory, it comes down to teaching the players what to do on the court. This is where the Basic Five moves come in. Players who can execute the moves of punching, dribble-pulling and dribble-rotating, reading the cuts to the open holes, screening the various areas, and know the proper method of attack in the inside game can go against zones with confidence. The book shows how players can be drilled to recognize their own openings so that your team can avoid being stereotyped in its attack. Everyone who has gone against good zone teams knows that it doesn't take long for the good teams to adjust to repeated zone patterns, that the offense has to keep adjusting and trying to confuse the defense. The best way to avoid this stereotyping is to have a system that has the kind of free-lance that allows the offense to read and adjust, forcing the defense to have to make its own adjustments or else change to a man-to-man.

For the times when the players need set patterns against the zones for one reason or another, or for the coach who does not want to utilize the free-lance aspect, there are dozens of offenses diagrammed in the book. The beauty of the system is that the offenses contain the Basic Five moves. When we move our players out of their free-lance game into one of our offenses, say the 1-4, they will still be utilizing Basic Five moves and the principles we have taught for attacking zones. But in the offense, we have determined the sequence ahead of time and have reduced the free-lance aspects greatly, though I feel it would be a serious mistake to eliminate free-lance possibilities altogether. Of course, players who have been taught the strong fundamental zone moves and know how to free-lance a little with them can really make a pattern work. The combination of pattern with intelligent free-lance is a winning formula in anybody's game.

In general the Basic Five exercises are to zone offense what such things as the shuffle cut, the back door cut, and the give and go are to man-to-man offenses. Most of the basic man-to-man offenses utilize one of the three aforementioned moves or a split the post or a baseline backdoor screen exercise. The combination in which each coach puts them together makes one offense just a little different from the next. This is what the Basic Five does. One takes the five best zone moves, teaches these exercises, and allows the players to use them either on their own as opportunities arise, or only in some of the patterns that the coach selects which will use the five moves anyway, or he can do what is suggested in the book; that is, he may allow some free-lance usage of the Basic Five and keep some plays for each specific type of zone defense.

I am grateful for those many fine coaches who one way or another have led me to know the zone moves that follow that I have decided are worthy to be called the Basic Five. At times their use of some of the moves or patterns shown inside cost us a victory, but again, the lessons were valuable even if the losses may have been unpleasant at the time. It is my hope that this book will add to the knowledge of the vexatious problem of attacking the zones.

Del Harris

Table of Contents

Coaching Basketball's Zone Offenses

1

Developing Effective Zone Offense Strategy

I just met a man who broke out of a state of depression long enough to tell me he was leaving his medical practice because, after several years of research, he was unable to find one medicine which would cure every sickness. He is the same man who had quit basketball coaching after failing to develop an offense that would beat every kind of defense.

Of course the foregoing incident is make-believe, but it alludes to a widely-accepted fallacy in basketball theory. The coaching journals are filled with diagrams of little offenses that are guaranteed by the author to be equally effective against both man-to-man and zone. While nothing is impossible, the reality of the situation more likely is that a coach found some certain moves with specific players that proved to be effective for a game or even a season against varying defenses. The point is that in each coach's exuberance to find that "one offense," he may let temporary success with a specific team influence him to think he has an answer for all men for all seasons. A simple example of this is the use of the high lob pass when a team has a seven-foot center. It's a fine move against all defenses—if you have a seven-foot center that can play and the other team does not. The offenses I have seen in many years of coaching require significant adjustment to meet the various defensive situations a team will meet per season.

The defensive game has become so complex over the years that the search for the "El Dorado" of one golden offense is only natural. It is admittedly very difficult to have one or two offenses for each different defensive attack. But, as in most problem-solving, the answer lies not on either extreme end of the pole. Most of today's coaches can remember when most teams used man-to-man exclusively. If they pressed, they pressed man-to-man. Fans tended to look upon a team that used zoning tactics as somehow inferior and its players as somewhat less than men. The real men, the real players, used man-to-man. I remember well hearing the downtown coaches advise, "No team will ever win the State High School Championship with a zone defense."

Yes, how times change. In fact, there was an era when virtually no one was using the zone presses; at the same time the accepted technique to beat any zone defense was to align the players in a 1-3-1 or into a side overload, pass the ball around, and attack the zone with the outside shot. As often as not, the uneducated zone defense would fail to adjust and the offense would be effective. But multiple defenses and offenses have added considerable depth to the modern game and have changed all that.

There are four styles of zone defense confronting today's coach, and innumerable variations to playing each of the four styles. These four styles are: 1) the standard containing zones; 2) the lane-playing zones; 3) the special zones; and 4) the pressing zones. Because of the significant differences in these defenses, it is not likely that one offensive pattern, or play would work with equal efficiency against each. It is just as unworkable to have 15 different patterns. Therefore, what I propose is a method which necessitates first identifying the defensive styles so that players may be aware of what they are facing, and, second, establishing the concepts for a system of attack. Naturally, we hope to do this with an economy of teaching effort and practice time.

The Four Styles of Zone Defense

Those familiar with my first book, *Multiple Defenses for Winning Basketball*, will recall that I explained the differences in each defensive type and sub-type or style. For our purposes here we will make only a brief descriptive reference to each of the four zone styles. It is of urgency that each coach and, ideally, each player be able to recognize the sometimes subtle shifts of styles in defense during a game which can create havoc for the offense.

The Standard Containing Zones. In this grouping fall all the basic traditional zone formations such as 1-2-2, 2-1-2, 1-3-1, 3-2, and 2-3 which have the primary purpose of keeping the ball out of the inside area. That is, these zones are meant to contain the high scoring area around the foul area and goal, forcing outside play as much as possible. The emphasis is for the players who are not guarding the ball to sag in towards the goal area and basket in order to deny passes to these spots. The ball may be pressured by one man when it is in the general scoring area, but every other defender is trying to contain the inside. Note the positions in diagram 1-1 as compared to 1-2 which shows the laning positions. (See p. 20.)

The Lane-Playing Zones. The laning zones operate from the same alignments as the containing zones. They differ in that the

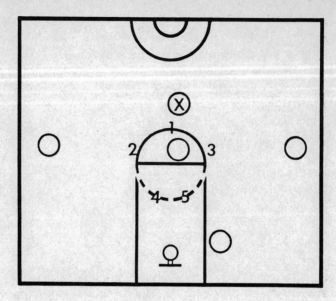

Diagram 1-1

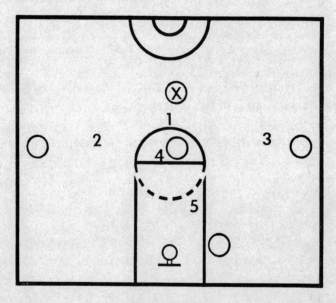

Diagram 1-2

laning defenders push out into the pass lanes adjacent to the
ballhandler in an effort to break up the passing and pattern
games. The containing zones shut off passes into the top
percentage area by dropping inside and being more conserva-
tive; but the lane zones are more aggressive and risk-taking.
They pressure the ball more heavily, force out into the adjacent
outside pass lanes with the two defenders on either side of the
ball, and hope that the other two defenders can keep the ball out
of the high and low posts. The entire defense originates a step or
two further from the goal than do the containing zones. To contain is to allow outside passing, while to lane is to try to break up
the passing and the pattern in an effort to confuse the offense. A
team which fails to adjust its offense when the defense goes from
containing to laning will experience difficulty penetrating and be
subject to frustration and turnovers.

The Special Zones. Primarily I speak of the "matchup" style
of zone here, but will include also such differentiations as the
box and one and the triangle and two. We can dismiss the latter
two by acknowledging the obvious, that the box or diamond
players (2-2 or 1-2-1) use a zone while one chaser plays man-to-
man on a key player. The triangle uses three men to zone while
two stick tightly to two key opponents. Of more significance is
the matching technique. This is a late development in defense
and involves an attempt to have a consistent one-on-one situation with a zone defense. It is man-to-man to a point in that each
defender has responsibility for one man within his general area.
It is not any specific player as in man-to-man, just whoever is
there at the given moment. He will not follow this man all over
the court but will use rules set by the coach to keep one-to-one
with someone all the time his team is on defense. The matchup
thus allows a lot of one-on-one coverage to stop overload tactics
and to put a crimp into the zone offensive patterns by keeping
players constantly matched up with the formations which are
changed by the offensive cuts and movements. Teams usually
match from a containing position, but it is possible to lane with it
as well. Although matching up is more difficult to teach, teams
who use it successfully can often prevent penetration all night
against teams who are unable to solve it.

The Pressing Zones. Here, obviously, I refer to the half- and full-court zone presses which employ two-timing, or trapping, on the ballhandler. Regardless of formation (1-2-2, 2-2-1, etc.), the zone presses will force a different tempo into the game and players must respond quickly, but cooly, or the zone press will take them right out of their game.

In summation, I believe it to be important to be able to identify each zone style and be prepared to combat each one which arises during a game situation. The team well-versed in zone identification and attack will be able to gain confidence in its ability to beat the defense and help eliminate the surprise or psychological advantages caused by zone play.

Establishing a System of Attack

So far I have expressed doubt that one offense can solve all defenses and affirmed that it is not practical to have different offenses for each defensive adjustment. What I suggest is to begin with a system of solid zone offense theory and then to establish a method of attack called *Organized Free-Lance*, which utilizes a fundamental core of zone maneuvers called the *Basic Five*. Players may use the Basic Five spontaneously to attack the various zone defenses. In addition, the coach will name specific plays or patterns to be used which employ any two or more of the Basic Five moves. In effect, once the offensive players know the zone style they are facing, they will first use the parts of the Basic Five best suited for that situation. But, any time the coach wants to change to put his team in a special pattern, he can tell his players to use the appropriate combination of the already-learned principles as an offense. More on this as we proceed, but the point is that every pattern or play used by the team will involve a combination of the Basic Five moves. The moves are free-lance when done in no specific sequence; any designated sequence becomes a pattern or play.

Having used zone defense considerably in my coaching, unfortunately I have witnessed many good zone-breaking tactics

employed by my opponents. I have been thankful for the lessons, if not for the losses. During these many seasons I have
found it easier to beat teams who had only two or three
stereotyped zone plays. Once we had practiced adjustments to
these moves, it became easier to contain the offense. The more
predictable the offensive pattern was, the easier it seemed to
prepare for an opponent. On the other hand, teams who were
more inventive, open-minded to free-lance possibilities, and
less stereotyped caused us more zone defensive problems.
Therefore, I wanted to use this style offensively rather than be
too predictable. The defensive coach who can use his matchup
zone well will be able to use scouting reports, or even just
directions given during halftimes or time-outs, to thwart re-
petitious pattern play. To avoid this stereotype, although we
utilize plays as previously noted, we have tried to familiarize our
team with the differing zone defenses and with principles of
counteracting moves to each style. The hope is that our players
will be able to *react to the defense.* In other words, instead of
allowing the defense the upper hand to adjust to our particular
set offensive move and force us to change to a new set, we hope
to present a more varied attack, Organized Free-Lance, which
adjusts to the defensive changes. Our idea is to *read* instead of
being read. The strategy is to help players identify the
opponent's defense quickly, suggest a beginning formation, and
then let them have the first chance to show that they can utilize
our moves in an intelligent manner on a free-lance, "read the
defense" basis. The players know they get the first opportunity.
Then, if we are not functioning properly, I will call upon a
specific set of our moves for them to use. This pattern will have a
specific name, and will in most cases still utilize the moves in the
Basic Five, but in a specified order rather than in free-lance.
Even in our patterns we encourge the opportune use of free-
lance, however. It is most enjoyable when the players are able to
beat the defense on their own. Players enjoy trying to stay ahead
of the opponent instead of using one play for a few minutes until
the opponent adjusts, then having to look to the bench to see
what trick play the coach wants to try for the next few minutes. A

real feeling of team play and togetherness between players and the coach often results.

Eight Points of Team Zone Offense

The basis for the Organized Free-Lance system is understanding the theory behind attacking the zones in the first place. Once the team understands the difference in zone styles, then knows the strategical theory behind team zone play and is drilled on techniques of execution, it is able to respond to changing game conditions. It is easier than it sounds, fortunately. Let us begin by listing the eight points for team strategy, keeping in mind that one point bears about equal weight to the others.

1. *The fundamental game.* Players need to have fewer offensive skills to play against zones. It is easier to get open against zones and they demand less one-on-one ability of an offensive player. Further, in my opinion, rebounding is more difficult for a team playing zone defense. For these reasons, to a degree, the opponents perform a favor by zoning. However, a team which neglects to develop its *passing game* will suffer greatly at the hands of a zone. While it is important to practice spot shooting, it is even more important as a first order of business to develop the overall passing game. It is unlikely that any of today's coaches spend enough time teaching and practicing the passing game. Good offense begins with good passing and it must be taught, drilled, and emphasized all season.

Possibly even more significant is the offensive rebounding game. A good offensive rebounding team takes inestimable pressure off of its shooters, its defense, and its offensive execution. Devoid of this vital factor a team must shoot a high percentage of its first shots, play a lot of time on the defensive end, and must really execute well offensively or else it will never get the ball inside for the close shots. Since the zone is weaker at blocking out, it may allow a better offensive rebound game. Still, the coach must, just as in the passing game, constantly emphasize the supreme value and dire necessity of both of these often-taken-for-granted fundamental aspects in order to get the most from his players. If the foregoing sentences were repeated five times, it would not stress these points strongly enough. The reason is, I suppose, that everyone wants to win with trick plays and forget just where it all has to begin—at the fundamental level.

2. *The fast break.* All right, so there are some successful coaches who never use the fast break. There are many ways to win a game and I do not criticize anyone just because he does not do it in a special way. Regardless, if a team's passing is soundly developed, it can gain a lot by using the break against the zone defense. It is a plus to force the other team to have to run back hard on defense. Because so many defensive players fail to get back quickly, why not capitalize on that weakness? If the offensive team can get the ball inside easily before the other team's bigger players arrive at the goal, it has earned an advantage. Once the defense is set, it will be harder to get the desired penetration. If a team can run and handle the ball well, the fast break is a fine extra tool to have.

3. *Put the defense in motion.* Whether a team employs a fast break or not, when it comes to a set position against an organized five-man defense, the offense must force defensive movement in order to create openings. A team cannot win consistently against good competition on the initial side of offensive entry. Anybody's defense, man-to-man or any style of zone, will be able to make the first defensive move often enough to hurt the offense. Teams who try to force outside shots on the first side or who try to force the ball inside all the time on the initial side are doing a favor to the defense. How many mistakes can a defense make in three to five seconds? When a zone offense is patient enough to move the ball to the reverse side, and even back to the original side or into the post and so on, it will force the defense into errors. Some good zones will follow the flow to the second side or even the third side without breaks occasionally. But for the team which has a good passing game, the odds are strongly in its favor that as the ball is moved, one or two

defenders will have a lapse in movement, leaving a crack in the wall of the defense upon which an alert offensive player can capitalize. Further, the offensive rebound game will be enhanced since the defense will not be allowed to center around the goal waiting for a shot right after the first pass. Believe me, from a defensive standpoint I have always preferred to play against teams who attacked our zones with only one or two passes. It is the patient team that has consistently given our teams more worry.

4. *Create passing lanes.* There are several factors involved in keeping passing lanes open and a team that has apparently developed a good passing game will at times go sour on its ballhandling because it neglects to fulfill good pass lane creation responsibilities. The offense with rare exception will function best by keeping spread, paying attention to player spacing, and thus keep the middle open for passing, cutting, and dribble-punches. The defense should generally be forced to cover as much floor space as possible. The offense that moves in too closely and fails to keep good pass lanes open will allow the defense to increase its efficiency. The less floor space to cover, the better the defense gets.

To keep pass lanes open the offense must: 1) keep wide on the wings when the ball is out front, and, stay deep at the point when the ball is on the side; 2) rotate on the periphery toward the ball when a teammate cuts inside between an outside player and the ball; 3) get wide on the side opposite the ball; and 4) step inside the laning zone players to create lanes inside the defense rather than be pushed out too far. We will elaborate on these points in the following paragraphs.

Keep wide on the wings and deep at the point. By staying wide at the wings the offense can pass the ball to a side easily and cause the first defensive shift. If the zone stretches wide to deny the wing, the lane for a pass inside or punch drive inside is more accessible. Exceptions could include a screening exercise or a cut to an open hole, of course. Meanwhile, the point man, or guard nearest the ball in a two-guard front, should stay very deep when the ball is on the wing or in the corner. This allows a quick reversal if the wing cannot play or pass inside. When the guard, or any player for that matter, has the ball, he may penetrate as deeply as he safely can. But the wise coach must guard against his team's natural tendency to pinch in too tightly, particularly against the containing zones. As I constantly remind my players, a team that "stays wide on the wing and deep at the point" will have three automatic benefits—freer outside movement of the ball which causes rapid defensive shifts, a more open middle for penetration, and the advantage of going against a defense that must cover considerable floor space from side to side in the scoring area.

Rotate on the periphery. Peripheral rotation is essential in order to keep the reverse passing avenues open. For example, if a wing man passes to a corner and cuts through to the goal, there will be no easy reverse avenue unless someone rotates into the general area of the vacated wing as in diagram 1-3. (page 28.) The point man, or the high post if desired, must cut very quickly to the open offensive spot, or else the ball may be trapped or at a minimum the offense will be slowed down, allowing the defense to adjust and rest. Remember the absolute importance of keeping a quick lane open toward the reverse side. Otherwise, almost anyone's zone will be able to follow a slowed down passing game as the ball moves slowly and aimlessly from side to side. It is the rapid reversal that causes defenders to fail in their shifting assignments.

Stay wide on the weak side. Keeping players who are on the side opposite the ball side will often evoke the response, "But, coach, I can get open at 15 feet if I just move in."

The only trouble is that by the time the ball gets to

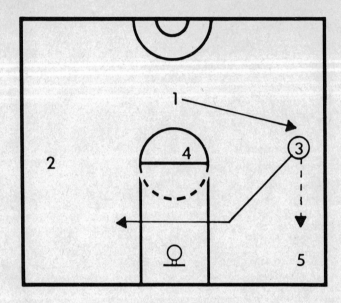

Diagram 1-3

him on the reverse, the defense will be able to make the shorter journey back to him and he is the one who helped make the defensive assignment softer. Of course, if a player opposite the ball sees an opening inside the zone between him and the ball, he is encouraged to cut to that defensive crease. But, as will be noted in the next chapter, he must cut back out to his wide wing spot if he fails to receive the ball or exercise the option to rotate to a teammate's spot if a teammate cuts out to the wide wing area that he just left. In general, staying wide on the side opposite the ball will serve the offense best and will increase the efficiency of the reverse passing game and set up possible cross-court passing tactics. Jamming up on the sides, except for a specific play which may call for a screen there, not only crowds up the offensive middle with members of both teams, but allows the defense the luxury of guarding a more limited floor space. The defense that has to follow the flow of the ball over a very narrow width is likely to cover it with fewer mistakes. On the other hand, a player receiving the ball on a reverse pass who is standing 20 to 22 feet wide has a better chance to receive the ball in the first place and can then capitalize on any defensive error. He may shoot if that is his range, or he may be able to beat the defender, who might be out of defensive body control as he scurries out to him, with a quick one-on-one move. Even if he is unable to capitalize on his own, he may be able to pass inside, to the corner or reverse the ball again to a deep point man and contribute to causing the defense some problems in one way or another.

Step inside the wide pass lanes. While it is good to be spread on offense, the lane zones can cause an offense to spread *too* far. Too much of a good thing can cause the offense to have trouble getting the ball inside as the pass lanes become overextended. While we want a wide offense in order to facilitate passing and inside penetration, we do not want to allow a lane zone to force our entire offense too far from the goal. Therefore, when a lane zone gets into the passing routes, it becomes important to have the wings backdoor into the approximate 25 to 20 foot range in order to get the ball inside the defense. The next chapter and later chapters will deal more specifically on this and how the posts and the man with the ball have options to penetrate the lane zones as well. But for now let it be said that just as the natural tendency of players going against the containing zones is to squeeze gradually in too close to the defense, their inclination against the lane zones is to keep spreading out wider and wider. Each must be avoided for the best results.

5. *Establish an inside game.* With the exception of when a coach has absolutely no inside players and the opponent is blessed with good shot-blockers, a team should establish an inside threat in their set attack. The team with no inside game must get some fast breaks, will have to be deadly in its medium and long range shooting game, and will have to hustle like crazy for every rebound and loose ball. We went 25-3 doing just those

things one season, but ideally, a team will have someone who can play reasonably well inside and it must take time to get the ball there once he becomes set. This means there must be a lot of high and low post passing and inside movement. Remember that a good passing team can get an outside shot anytime it wants it. In International Basketball with the 30-second clock, I always ask my players to wait until after the number 15 shows on the clock to shoot a 20 foot or longer shot. We can get that long shot whenever we want it, but unless we spend time probing inside we will never get the short shots that can produce baskets and fouls, and which force all the opponents to be in the defensive game. A team that tries to shoot too quickly or with too many outside shots plays right into the hands of the defense. Once an inside threat is fixed, the defense must keep moving in and out, playing a more honest defense and increasing the chances for defensive errors and offensive openings.

6. *Keep offensive pressure in the high and low post.* In order to effect an inside game the offense must continuously explore possible openings in the high and low posts. Obviously, if the low post frees himself, the offense can get a high percentage shot, provided there is no shot-blocker imminent. Still, it is quite an offensive advantage if the team can get the ball under the goal. Sometimes underestimated, but of utmost importance, is the high post pass. By high post, I mean *extremely* high. It is the natural inclination of most players in that area to try to get open at the foul line. However, players in the high post area should know that they must regularly step out as high as the top of the circle and occasionally a step or two higher to get the ball. An up-and-down movement from the foul line to the extreme high post is vastly superior to just standing in one spot.

The main benefit to passing the ball into the high post is that it puts the defense in a situation where there is no weakside help. The high post man can pass directly under or to either wing or corner area. In fact, we instruct our post men to turn, look under, and then look opposite every time they receive the ball. So vital is the high post pass that the coach can insist that every third or fourth pass go into the high post. High post penetration is basic to playing against all types of zones.

7. *Penetrate the zone.* I have used the word penetrate many times already, for it is so integral to effective zone attack. A quick review of the first six suggestions will show that many of the points already made facilitate penetration of the zone. Still, it is important to include a specific statement regarding it. Keep in mind that the position of seventh place in the listing is not indicative of its significance. Penetration means getting the ball inside the defense, behind at least one of the defenders. There are five ways to get the ball into the defensive interior. They are: 1) the direct pass; 2) the drive; 3) the dribble-punch; 4) the dribble-pull and pass; and 5) cutting to the inside holes.

The direct pass. This is the simplest way to penetrate, but good zone defense will make it difficult to accomplish. Therefore, I tell my players that anytime they see an easy direct opening to pass the ball to either the high or low posts, forget all else they had in mind, and capitalize immediately on the opportunity. It is that vital that we get the ball there as often and as safely as we can. But be sure it is safe.

The drive. We want our outside players to look for the drive first upon receiving the ball. Even inside, they must be aware of any opportunity to take the ball a step or two strongly into the goal. We want to use driving tactics against any kind of defense. If the player has an immediate one-on-one or maybe even a one-on-nobody, he should make a controlled drive to the goal. I say the word "controlled" so that if the drive is sealed off, the driver will not commit the offensive foul, but will either outmaneuver the defense or give the ball up to a teammate. This is the prime reason our teams have averaged shooting 200 more free throws per season than the opposition. A driver will draw fouls. Be clear that I am not talking about aimless dribbling or careless drives into a pack of two or three defenders. One must insist on legitimate drives just as he does open shots and good passes to open inside people. To force the offense is to ask for problems.

The dribble-punch. The ballhandler must look for the two opportunities to use punching. The first incidence is when he has the ball and the defense tries to split him without either one of the two nearest defenders actually taking him straight up, as in diagram 1-4. When the ballhandler, 1, sees a gap between the defense, he punches right into that gap with one or two bounces. He will then choose to shoot if no one covers him or else will pass the ball to the nearest open offensive player, usually the player nearest the zone defender who moved to cover the ball. To fail to penetrate in this situation is to allow the defense to guard the four offensive players who do not have the ball with five men, because there is actually no defender on the ball. The other use of punching is to drive at an angle right toward another defender, even when the ballhandler has a man straight up on him as in diagram 1-5. The point man is covered and the defense is matched up, making it hard to get the offense going. So the point dribbles two or three quick bounces right at or preferably a step inside of the wing defender. He can then pass the ball to his own wing man, 3, as the defender flexes to stop his apparent drive.

The dribble-pull and pass. This technique involves bouncing the ball and moving in a lateral position one or two steps in order to create a better passing angle into either of the post areas. In diagram 1-6 player 1 bounces two steps laterally toward the sidelines, and in so doing, facilitates a pass into the high post. In fact, one of our plays which will be discussed later involves exactly this move combined with the post taking a step or two out into the extreme high post area. The latter move is not always necessary. Of course a wing can use the dribble-pull to make it easier to drop the ball into the low post as well. The dribble-pulling helps break the direct line of three in a row—the ballhandler, his defender, and the intended receiver. Diagram 1-7 shows a line of three in a row which makes it tough for the passer to get the ball inside. By pulling the defender and instructing the inside people to

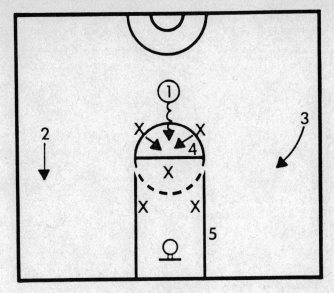

Diagram 1-4

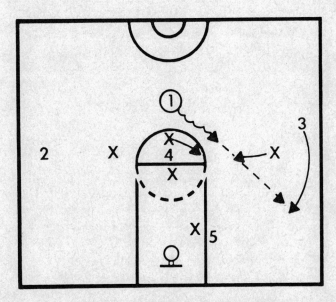

Diagram 1-5

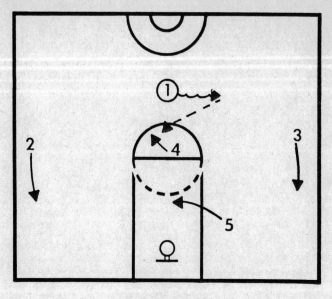

Diagram 1-6

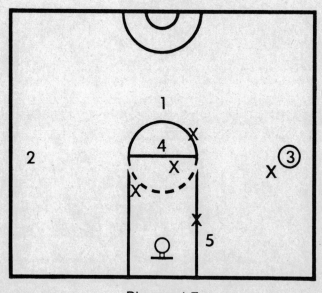

Diagram 1-7

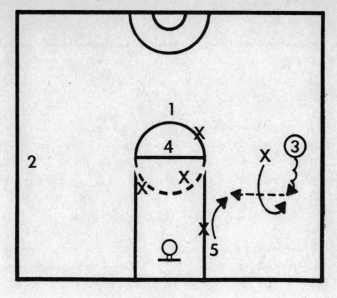

Diagram 1-8

move a half-step opposite any dribble-pull move, a new pass lane is opened as in diagram 1-8. (See drills.)

Cut to the inside holes. When a player without the ball sees a path to the ball inside the defense, he should move to it. If he can get the ball, penetration is accomplished. If not, he must keep moving. He should make a circle cut or a "V" cut back to near where he originated rather than stand inside and jam up the offense. Players must be alert to read these openings as they occur, whether they are a part of a set play or not. It is this kind of defensive opening that the free-lance system thrives on. (See drills.)

8. *Use some man-to-man techniques.* As you read you will see that I like to use more than just the one-on-one drive against zones that the man-to-man offenses employ. Against the match-ups and the box and one kinds of zones we often revert strictly to our man-to-man offense. But in free-lance zone offense the basic moves of screening and the give-and-go have a definite place.

Screening may be used in many instances. The high post may ɔcreen for the point and then roll or pop out to the top of the circle. The wing man may pinch the baseline defender to allow a cutter to pop out to the corner to get a pass. Or the wing opposite the ball may squeeze in to screen for the point man for a weak-side two-man game as the ball reverses from the wing to the point. The posts should be encouraged to screen for each other as often as they desire. (We will discuss these fully, later.)

Another man-to-man move is the automatic give-and-go which occurs when the high post passes to a wing or corner. He passes to the wing-corner area in diagram 1-9 and then cuts right to the goal looking for a return pass. It is surprising how often this one move can return dividends in a game.

The main point in using man-to-man principles in the zone offense goes back to the fact that there are just so many man-to-man defensive principles being utilized by the zone defenses. It only follows that some man-to-man moves would prove to be effective.

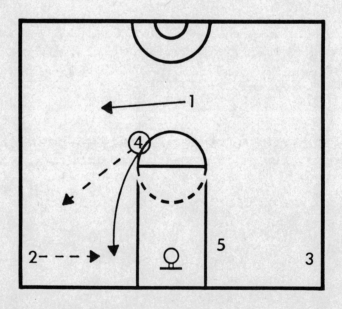

Diagram 1-9

Special Strategy Against Zones

Some techniques employed by coaches against man-to-man teams are overlooked when the same coach faces a zone defense. Just as in the man-to-man situation, the offense should try to steer the ball into the area of a defensive player who is a key performer, especially if he is laden with fouls. Against a team that is going to play 40 minutes of zone, the offense can start early in taking the ball to the star player's side. Or, it may take the ball to the weaker defensive side, when that can be determined. Or, it may take the shots on the side of the opponent's best rebounders, since rebounds tend to go opposite the shot. With any kind of a lead the offense may elect to pull the ball out on the floor and force the team who desires to play zone to stretch that zone and allow openings or to change to a man-to-man, a defense it did not prefer to play in the first place. While this is not as effective when there is a 30-second clock, it is still of some use.

In summation this chapter reveals some team principles of zone play. These are not offenses or plays but they form the theory behind which the Organized Free-Lance system, or, in my opinion, any system, may best operate. The next chapter will give suggestions for the individual in zone play for performing the techniques which make the principles and patterns effective.

Suggestions for Team Play Against the Zone Defenses

1. Have patience with the set offense. Try to get the ball inside. Give the defense time to make a mistake.
2. Move the ball and move the players. You cannot win against good teams on the first side. Face the goal and give the cutters two seconds to move before giving the ball up.
3. Every third or fourth pass must get into the post area.
4. The posts must rotate positions at least every three

passes. Or, one could say every three or four seconds the posts must move.

5. Wait for the outside shot. You can get it anytime.

6. Pass the ball inside whenever you can, but only when a man is in good position to receive the ball and make a positive move with the ball. Don't force the ball to a covered man.

7. Bounce pass all passes into the traffic areas.

8. Snap your passes. Do not float them.

9. Keep spaced from the rest of your teammates. Be wide on the wings and deep on the point.

10. Keep pass lanes open. Move to the ball when you must.

11. When you receive the ball from 18 feet out, look for the drive, then the pass inside. Look for the open long shot only when it is appropriate.

12. When you get the ball inside of 18 feet, look for the shot, then the drive or the pass inside to another. Anytime the drive is there, you should take it.

13. Control your body on the drive.

14. Penetrate with cuts, passes, and drives. Get the ball behind a defender and go to work.

15. Rebound, rebound, rebound.

2

Coaching Zone Offense Individual Techniques

The individual techniques of this chapter will apply some of the theoretical principles of team play from the first chapter. This chapter will explain some of the individual moves that make the theory for effective team zone offense work. The following chapter will demonstrate how team theory and individual techniques are combined to form the Organized Free-Lance System. These three aspects are separate, yet are so interrelated that there is necessarily a good bit of overlapping. In the end it should be clear how good theory and sound technique go together to produce an effective offensive attack against the zones.

There are many techniques that apply to playing any position on the floor against the zones. For instance, all players must be able to pass the basketball. Passing should be made toward the *outside* of the defense in order to help prevent steals—zone defenders are often more eager to try to cut off passes since they feel they have better support behind them if they fail to make the steal. Players anticipating a pass on the periphery should face the ballhandler and plant the inside foot (foot nearest the goal) with the toes pointing as directly toward the basket as possible. By doing this the receiver need only complete his pivot in order to square around to a triple-threat position. Thus a quicker drive or shot or pass inside can be accomplished before the defensive pressure can become too great. Another helpful hint for all zone attackers is to look at the goal frequently when receiving the ball. Although we insist that our players who receive the ball on the periphery look first for the drive, then the pass inside, it is still wise to look up often at the basket. If players look to the goal, the defense will tend to tighten up on the ball, making the drive easier, and forcing the defender to play the man as a threat. On the other hand, a player who never looks at the goal gives the defender an immediate advantage because he knows that shooting is not one of the options against which he has to protect. Furthermore, players who are accustomed to looking at the goal frequently will realize more quickly when they are open in the higher percentage ranges. I have so often seen players receive the ball in an open situation who realize it a second too late because they did not have the habit of looking to the goal.

Any player may have to try to feed the ball inside. It seems that the tendency is for players to throw lob passes or other air passes into the posts. A coach would probably do himself and his players a favor by demanding that every pass that goes into the post areas be a bounce pass. Even though this would eliminate the "andy-over" lob pass, it would also eliminate a lot of errors. Even if the coach allows the lob in certain conditions, he should insist that the inside pass be made only when it is a positive offensive move (that is, be sure that the post man is open to receive the ball and has room to make a move). Too many times players throw the ball into a pack inside when the best thing the post man can do is to make a good catch just to keep the ball from being stolen. Give the ball inside as often as the posts are open; just be sure they are open. Insist on open shots, open drives, and open inside passes.

Many coaches get upset at cross-court passing. However, if the offense will remember the principle of staying wide, particularly on the side opposite the ball, the hard cross-court pass can be a very effective tool. Again, one of the principles of team offense is to keep the avenue to the reverse side open. The quickest way to get the ball to the opposite side is one hard pass, rather than two. Of course, it is important to notice the use of the term "hard pass." A soft, hanging pass will not get the job done. Players should drill the two-hand overhead pass in their passing drills because this is the kind of pass that has the best chance of getting across the court. If there is any question on the part of the passer as to whether he can complete the pass across the court, he should hold onto the ball. The long passes must be sure ones. Ball possession is of utmost importance.

Eight Specific Techniques for All Players

Points listed under this heading emphasize individual responsibility and technique in achieving several of the items of zone attack principles stressed in the first chapter. Once players can identify what the defense is doing, there are several ways any individual may respond in order to get the offense moving effectively. The following list offers when and how to utilize eight effective moves for the offense.

1. *Break the matchup by cutting.* Each player should constantly be looking for opportune moments to cut to the goal or to open spots in the zone between himself and the ball. A player should not cut just for the sake of it or to look busy, however. The two prime times to cut are when a player sees a gap in the

defense and when he realizes the defense has a perfect matchup
on the offense. The first chapter alluded to the first instance,
those times when the defense has applied man-to-man principles to the point that it is lined up head-on with the offense.
With no cuts or other attempts to make an offensive move, the
offense will do no better than a shot with a man right on the
shooter. One way to break this is to cut to a hole, forcing the
zone to shift in order to get lined up with the offense again.

As long as the offense is able to get players open in the gaps
or in the post areas, it is in a good position to free someone
without many cuts and, therefore, in those situations not much
cutting should be done. Just use good passing in those instances.
But as soon as a player (usually the ballhandler will notice it first)
realizes that the defense is lined right up with the offense, he
should pass the ball and execute a cut through the defense. This
forces the defense to adjust in order to remain matched up. At
this moment another player may be able to capitalize on the shift
in the defense to free himself in the post or in a crease or gap
made by a defensive error. Although it does not have to be the
ballhandler who initiates the cut, the give-and-go effect is the
one normally employed because the ballhandler is usually the
first to realize the situation due to the difficulty in finding someone to pass to easily.

In diagram 2-1 player 2 realizes everyone is matched up and
elects to pass and cut through, looking for a return pass. When
he gets into the baseline area, he looks and reads the defense to
see where he should go next. If 4's defense stays on 4, 2 is open
in the corner. If 4's defender slides off and lets the man on 2 shift
to cover 4, player 2 will read that and cut to the opposite corner
to form an overload on that side. These are good examples of
reading a defense and responding to what is seen. Each player
must work on his ability to see and react to the defensive holes to
make all of the zone moves more effective.

2. *Rotate to fill in the pass lanes.* In order to have a coor-
dinated cutting game, it is essential that players be alert to fill in
the spot vacated by the offensive man who cuts from the perimeter. *Immediately* someone must cut to the vacated spot either

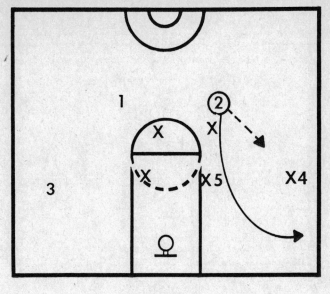

Diagram 2-1

from the next peripheral position over from the ball or from the high post area in order to keep the reverse pass lane open.

Diagrams 2-2 and 2-3 show first the perimeter man cutting to fill in the area opened by 2's cut and then the post man 5 filling it in the next diagram. In each instance player 3 must react to fill in the open spot in front of him in order to keep the offense tied together. Naturally, this is a situation that calls for the wing to leave his wide position so as to keep the reverse lane open in diagram 2-2 and to keep high post pressure in diagram 2-3. When one player cuts, it is the signal for every player to be alert to make his corresponding move, depending on what he can read from what the defense does and what his other teammates do. These cuts should be made quickly. Slow cuts will hurt the offense seriously. (See p. 44.)

3. *Keep moving in the posts.* Players in the post or even perimeter players who cut into the post area must keep moving in the interior of the defense. This is true against all types of

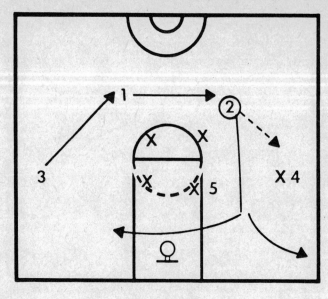

Diagram 2-2

Diagram 2-3

zoning. To get into that area and stand will not only fail to help that person get open, it will hamper the inside game for the entire team. Post men should shift from high post to low post and vice-versa by circle rotating, by screening each other, or by crossing (making an X) on the reversal of the ball every third pass or every three seconds. A post man who fails to change position high and low will be an easy defensive target. Even if the abilities dictate that one of the post players is better down low and the other up high, unless they move, each will be seriously handicapped in doing anything in the area in which he functions best. The posts are to have the ball every third or fourth pass and to get this done they must move a lot, remembering to cut quite high to get open, especially when the guard or guards seem to be looking for a place to throw the ball.

If a perimeter player sees an apparent hole in the defense and cuts to the defensive interior but does not receive the ball, he should not even wait for three passes. He should either circle cut, go on through, or form a V-cut to get out. Of course, if he sees a new area open in a corner, for example, he may move to it. Diagrams 2-4, 2-5, and 2-6 show the circle, the V-cut, and going ahead to the open hole respectively. (See pp. 46-47.)

4. *Use the punch when a hole opens in front of the ball.* Each player should be instructed to use the dribble wisely. The old idea of zone offense was that the dribble had no place in it. I agree that dribbling can get out of hand in any offensive attack, but that is no reason to eliminate it all together. As noted in the first chapter, many of the ways to penetrate the defense involve the use of the dribble, at least a modified dribble, as in the case of the punch and the dribble-pull. Of course, it is easy to remember that we use the drive to the goal as our first option with our players, as well. Certainly players must practice these techniques in order to perfect them and simple three-on-three drills can be set up to teach punching and the dribble-pull. (See drills.)

Diagrams 2-7 and 2-8 show players 1 and 2 punching into defensive gaps respectively. Here are two points very crucial to execution. First, the ballhandler on the punch must not punch

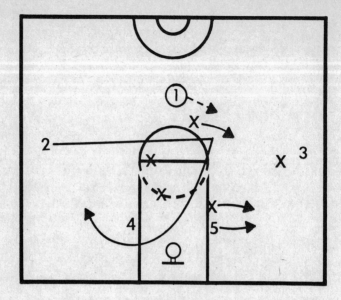

Diagram 2-4

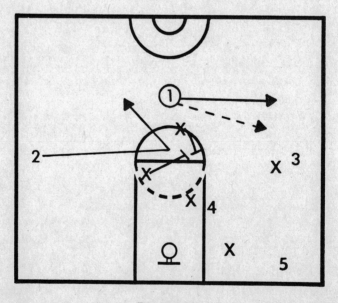

Diagram 2-5

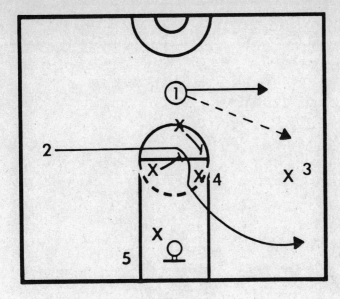

Diagram 2-6

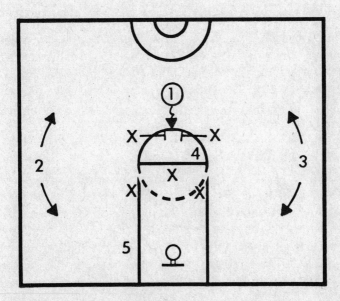

Diagram 2-7

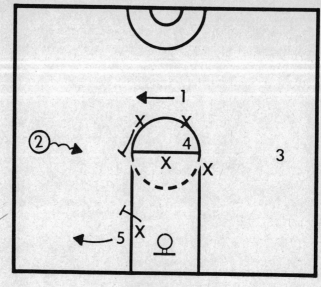

Diagram 2-8

right up against the defense. He must punch only one or two bounces and pick up the ball before he gets heavy defensive coverage. If he penetrates too far and allows himself to feel heavy defensive pressure, he will not be able to pass the ball off well. As soon as the offensive player has made the defense commit to him, he should pick up the ball and look to drop the pass to an open player, usually the player nearest the defender who flexes toward the ball. Of course, if no one covers him on the punch, he has an open shot.

The second point of the technique is often overlooked, but is essential to the consistent success of the original punch move. Notice in diagrams 2-7 and 2-8 that both perimeter players nearest the ball move *laterally* a step or two in either direction when the ballhandler punches into the gap. It is important that the adjacent players resist the temptation to move a step or two forward toward the goal at the same time the punch is made. While it seems natural to do so, a forward move negates the

punch in two ways. It makes it difficult for the ballhandler to
pass the ball off because it puts the defender more into the pass
angle. Further, it allows the man who flexes to cover the ball to
have a shorter recovery route to get back to the ball if the
puncher passes off to the man stepping in.

In the diagrams players 2 and 3 are shown cutting either *up*
or *down*, but not *in* more than just slightly. The choice of either
up or down depends on what the offense reads as he looks at the
defense. By moving down in diagram 2-7, players 2 and 3 increase the distance for either front defender to get back to them
if they move toward the ball, but also make the pass angle a little
tougher by putting them in a three-man line with the ball and
the defender on the ball. If 2 or 3 gets the ball, he will be open
or will have to be covered by a back man, which will then open
up the low post momentarily. If player 2 or 3 chooses to move up
instead of down, he shortens the pass angle, but the defender
can get to him more easily. Still, the ease and speed with which
he can receive the pass will give him extra time to set for the
shot.

A special point of note is the movement of 5 in diagram 2-8.
Player 2 punches into a gap he caused by faking baseline and
then going into the hole his defender made by overshifting.
Player 1 on the outside can choose to flare wide or step back just
as players 2 and 3 could do in the previous diagram. A low post
rule we use on all our offenses applies here to 5: if a man
punches or drives into the lane, the low post man must take a
step or two out on the baseline and look for a drop pass. The
other part of the rule, though not shown here, is for the low post
to take two steps up in an angle toward the wing if a man
punches or drives baseline side. This rule will serve one of two
purposes in every instance. It will either open up the post man
for a short jumper if the defense stays inside to cover the ballhandler, or it will give the driver more room if the defense clears
out to follow the post man. This one or two step pull move
coincides with the idea of moving the peripheral players when a
player punches. Everyone should adjust to the movement of the
ball. Thus, the movement makes it more open for the ball-

handler to drive, pass, or shoot and forces the defense to keep playing heads up instead of being able to gain an advantage as the offense and defense come together in a crowded area. Three-on-three drills for this purpose will quickly educate the players as to the efficacy of these moves. (See drills.)

In concluding the discussion of the techniques of punching the ball, I want to add a very significant last item. The coach should not only instruct the ballhandlers to look to punch when they have a good opportunity (not every time one gets the ball, however) but also teach that once the punch is made and the ball is passed off, the puncher should immediately jab back out to where he came from. He should realize that the move is actually a combination "punch-in and jab-out" move. If he punches in and stays, he helps the defense by crowding the area. Besides, he may set himself up for a quick return pass by jabbing out in the event that the defense is able to recover to the man he passed to before the new ballhandler can make an effective offensive move. At any rate, he gives the new ballhandler a clearer path by jabbing back out. This coordinates with the principle of keeping the interior open, of not standing on the inside.

5. *Dribble-pulling to help passing penetration.* When the offense is having difficulty moving the ball inside because the defense is moving and matching up the inside movement well, the ballhandler can still get the ball to people inside by executing a quick dribble-pull exercise with an inside player. The dribble-pull is quite easy to execute, but like so many moves, if not done correctly, it is of little use. Diagrams 2-9 and 2-10 show two dribble-pull exercises. In the first of the diagrams, 1 has the ball and bounces two quick bounces to his left. If the defense does not cover him, he is in a gap and can continue on a punch or drive. Normally, the defense will go with him. Just as 1 picks up the ball, 4 takes two quick steps up and away from the ball. If he goes too soon the defender on him or on 2 will get to him. The same will occur if he goes too lazily. A quick step or two and a pivot toward the ball will give him an opening for a shot on the pass from 1 or possibly he will be able to pass under after the

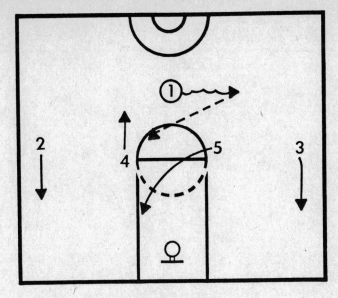

Diagram 2-9

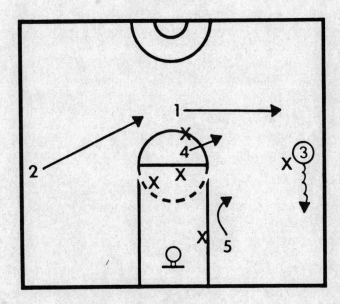

Diagram 2-10

cross move of 5 or the drop moves of 2 and 3 to the corner. Going along with our system, if 4 feeds 2 or 3 he will cut to the goal. This play will appear later as one of our key moves against zone defenses. When done crisply, it is tough for the defense to cover.

Diagram 2-10 shows wing 3 pulling his defense and the adjustments of 4 and 5 along with the perimeter players to the movement of the ball. Player 3 pulled to try to set up a better pass angle to the posts. If he is unable to feed 4 or 5 he can reverse to 1 and go baseline to the other side, while 4 and 5 can cross on the reverse, putting a lot of pressure on the defense to readjust.

6. *Use the drive as a deadly weapon against aggressive zones.* As aforementioned, we stress looking for the drive against all defenses. One must be sure to stress the difference between driving and just dribbling the ball because careless bouncing will slow down the ball movement and allow the defense to rest and to adjust. The player who overuses the drives, punches, or dribble moves can stop the offense so severely that he is as much a bother to the offense as the man who takes poor shots. Encourage open drives under control, remembering that "control" means being able to avoid the offensive foul and to see open teammates. The intelligent use of the drive will help the penetration and the foul possibilities tremendously. Make those inside people have to play defense!

7. *Use the dribble-rotate to pull the zone out of matched positions.* Diagram 2-11 shows one of the dribble moves which will appear again later in the book. For now, the important thing is that the dribble-rotate move is distinguished from a pull by the fact that a pull is only one or two lateral bounces, whereas the dribble-rotate is a dribble from one offensive slot to another with a complete perimeter rotation.

Point man 1 is having trouble moving the ball to the sides or is faced with a defense that is getting matched up easily against the offense. To create defensive adjustment and force his offense to move, as well, he dribbles to the wing while 2 and 3 rotate a full slot quickly. The posts time their cuts so as to put the most pressure on the defense (more on their moves later in the dis-

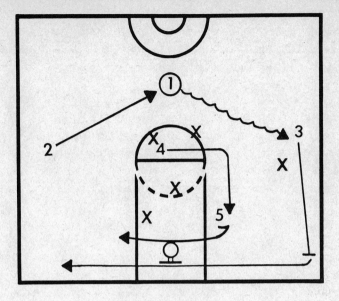

Diagram 2-11

cussion on post play). Player 1 has recognized that the defense is in matched positions, so to create a defensive problem, he rotates the offense with his dribble. The defense has to rotate with him or else to shift as each player cuts. The dribbler should move quickly to a spot just *above* the site where the wing was standing. If he goes slowly, the defense can adjust easier. If he tries to go inside, he will meet resistance—and anyway, this would constitute a punch move, not a dribble-rotate. Player 1 should look for a quick reversal if he cannot get the desired outcome on the first side. Player 3 quickly roves the base to put extra pressure on the reverse side.

This is a good exercise for the ballhandler when he feels his own players have begun to stand around on the offense. It automatically forces all the players to respond to him and the defense must regard his move as well. It will be effective from any formation and against all the zones.

8. *Screen the zones just as if they were man-to-man.*

When evaluating the use of screens against the zones, keep in mind that many man-to-man offenses will be relatively effective against zones, especially the matching or containing zones that tend to fall into basic matched positions. The more man-to-man a team uses in its zone defense, the more effective the man-to-man offense logically will be. Adding the uses of the dribble moves and some of the zone offense theory to the regular man-to-man offenses can be of great benefit to the offensive team. Laning tactics will put a damper on most man-to-man offensive patterns however.

In going from screening players who are playing against the offense with a man-to-man to those who are playing zone, the offense will have to adjust to screening players who are not necessarily right on the player for whom the screener is supposed to screen. He will have to seek the person in the defense who will logically try to cover the man the screener is trying to free. Obviously, the defender will not always be conveniently lined up right in front of the screener's teammate who is supposed to cut off the screen as in the man-to-man. I would emphasize that the screener always screen and then *look right back to the ball*. He may be able to get the ball himself by merely stepping back to the ball, or by rolling to the goal. Instead of rolling to the goal, he may be open simply by just popping back out away from the goal a step or two and receive a pass for an outside shot. Also, if a man screens for a man away from the ball, he should set the screen according to the ball position. That is, if the ball is above the player being screened, he should set his screen high on the defensive side of the player, but if the ball is below the player, he should set the screen on the low side of the defender.

Diagrams 2-12 through 2-16 show some of the screening possibilities mentioned in the first chapter. In diagram 2-12 we see a baseline continuation move. The screens are set on the high side and the screener turns right back to the ball just as he screens to see if he is open himself. Player 3 continues on across with the reversal of the ball. Post man 4 looks to feed 3 or 2 as 2 screens and looks. Player 2 can continue right off of 5 or the offense can employ another move at this point. Diagram 2-13

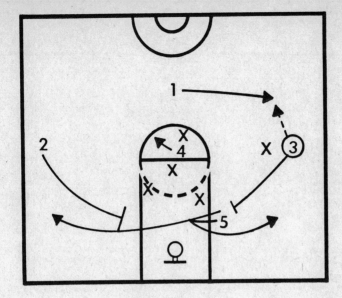

Diagram 2-12

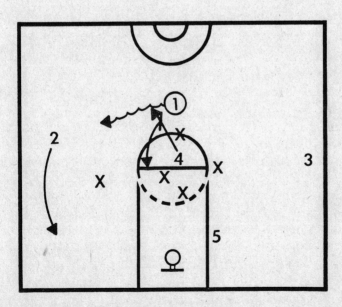

Diagram 2-13

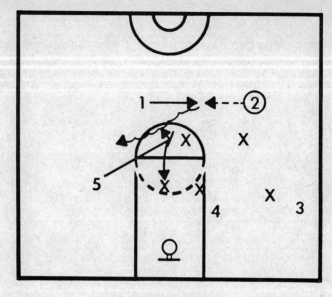

Diagram 2-14

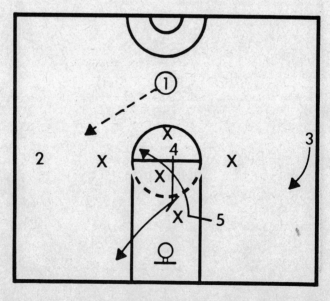

Diagram 2-15

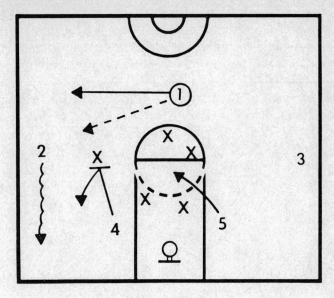

Diagram 2-16

shows a simple point screen with 4 using his option to roll or to pop out.

Diagram 2-14 shows the regular weakside two-man game caused by the offense pulling the defense into a straight matchup position. In diagram 2-15 the posts execute a screen and look move while 2-16 shows a post screen for the wing. Thus, when it is desirable, the offense can put the defense into positions where it has to execute man-to-man defense whether it wants to or not. (See drills.)

A final hint when using a man-to-man offense against a zone is to have the players be sure to continue their cuts even when they can find no one to screen on a given cut.

Special Techniques for Guard or Point Play

Every player should be able to execute the points listed in the foregoing discussion of the eight techniques because any player may find himself in a position where he will have to use those techniques often. And although several players may find themselves rotated even into the point spot, the men who have principal responsibility in this area should know a special trick or two about their jobs. Their biggest responsibility is to keep the offense moving, to avoid stagnation. This is important because a standing offense can be a sitting duck for the defense. If the guards can force the defense to keep in motion, one of the defenders is going to make a mistake upon which the offense can capitalize. The guards must have the mental control to continue looking for other people to be open in order to get them the ball and yet, at the same time, must be able to recognize when they are open themselves for a shot or drive. I always tell our play-making guards that while they are in that position, they are different from the rest of the players in that one point. You will recall that I mentioned I want my players to look first for the drive from the outside; however, the point guard must put that second on his list. He looks first to move the ball to open people and still must see when that really good drive, punch, or shot is there for him. He must look for the other man's opening, yet quickly recognize his own.

While keeping the offense in motion is essential, the guard must also constantly have the idea of our goal—to score by penetration—in his mind. All players need to know this, but the floor leader has to help everyone else when they forget. He looks to make penetrating passes, will punch, initiate dribble-pulls and rotates, etc. He must be aware of the rule of getting the ball into the posts every third or fourth pass. The wings have to be aware of all these items as well, but the guards bear the greater responsibility.

To keep the offense flowing and to enhance the chances for penetration, the guards have a major role in reading the defense so as to determine when the defense has them matched up or has begun to play in the lanes. That is, if the defense is in a good one-on-one matchup, nobody is going to get absolutely open until a move is made to force an adjustment. When a guard sees that the defense is covering the offense well, he may initiate a cut and then read where it seems best for him to cut—either to the ball side or to the side opposite. If the defense is in the pass lanes, he will have to look for all the opportunities he can see and ones he can create to get the ball into the inside of the lanes. He will have to remind his wings to backdoor, his posts to move even more aggressively in the high post area, and will have to initiate some dribble-pulls of his own to help penetration. He will have to be very alert for more punching possibilities and may even have to call set plays which are used for the laning defenses. In other words, the guard must exert himself to keep the offense in gear. He can do a lot more than a screaming coach can do during the game, but he has to be taught.

A little trick that some good front men employ is the fake reversal. While we insist on keeping the reverse lanes open and stress that the offense will not succeed consistently on the original side of entry, a good play at times is for the guard to catch the ball from the wing or corner on the reverse and then fake a pass or even bounce one time in the direction of the reverse and then come right back with a pass to the same side. Against a team that is really hustling and making its defensive shifts hard, the fake reverse can be quite a help to the offense.

When the guards do not have the ball, they must remember not to drift in toward the circle and jam up the rest of the offense. When they have the ball, they are on their own for drives and punches. But without the ball they must remain deep in order to free the high post and to allow for quick reversing of the ball. They should hustle toward the ballhandler on the wing or in the corner so that the pass back to the reverse side is easy, reducing the risk of interception. By staying back deep and in a good passing angle with the ball, the guards will not only help in keeping the rapid flow going and in reducing errors, but will also be in the best position to assume their big job of defensive balance as well. Many teams are able to run really well out of a zone, especially if they have two domineering rebounders. The other three men can run out quickly and really put pressure on the other end rapidly. Therefore the guards have to remember their duty to help check the running game. We always designate our two guards to be responsible for fast break balance no matter where they are when the shot is taken, however. The deepest one from the goal has deep responsibility, the other has long rebound and stop the ball responsibilities.

Special Techniques for Post Play

Since the post area is the danger zone for the defense, the area it must protect if it is going to survive, the first job of the offensive post player is to get open. The offense wants to get the ball inside. The offense wants to penetrate and the pass inside is one of the main methods of doing this. There are three things the posts must do well if they are to get open very often against the good zone teams. *First*, the high post player must make up his mind that he is not going to stand on the free throw line all night. He will have to move five to ten feet further out on the floor than the foul line to get the ball. When he receives the ball anywhere in the high post, he *must always* perform the one move that makes every zone suffer—turn and face the goal. At this time any player in the low post area can cut across in front of the goal in a sincere effort to get himself open. The fact that the high post has received the ball anywhere from 18 to 25 feet from the goal will help open up the middle for his pass down to the low post or for a drive to the goal. It is difficult to overemphasize the value of this one exercise. It is so valuable a move that a three-man drill should be used every few days for this exercise during the season. The high post pass receiver must get the habit of getting open, turning and looking under the goal, and then to the opposite wing or corner area. All the time, if he sees his driving path open up, he must know to take it to the basket. (See drills.)

Second, the post players should change positions at least after every three passes. They may mix up the way they do this by allowing the high post man to initiate the moves or may use another key. They may circle, simply rolling in a circular motion toward the flow of the ball or they may screen each other. An especially good move on the reversal of the ball after both posts have moved to the ball side is to cross (make an X) as the ball is reversed to the other side. Diagrams 2-17 and 2-18 show circling and crossing. The main point is to avoid post play that involves the two post men moving only laterally across the free throw area. It's so easy to guard players who do this that the defense inside can practically take the night off. The only exception I know of is when a team has such a dominating giant inside that he can get open consistently on his stature alone. The years a coach has this type of player, he can get by on a lot less coaching technique.

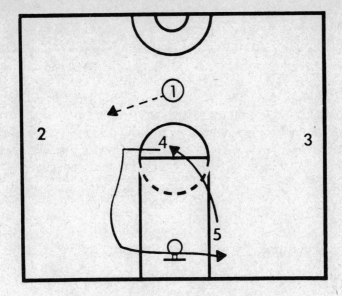

Diagram 2-17

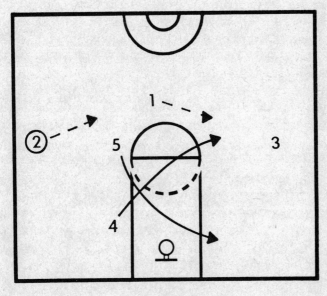

Diagram 2-18

Third, in order to get open easier inside, the posts should realize that they are a two-man team. They must watch each other and move accordingly. When one is not open, he should cut or go screen the other in order to help him get open. They should talk during a game to let each other know how each feels he can help themselves and the team. By doing this they can remind each other of their responsibility to keep motion alive on the inside and can avoid ending up with both of them standing in the same position with only one defensive man covering the two. They must help each other in every way; they are a team within a team.

When an outside player initiates a dribble-rotate move, the posts must time their cuts on their own in order to roll down into positions where they can get open as the defense adjusts. Also, if the outside players fail to adjust (or at times just for variation) on the dribble moves, the high post must pull out to fill the vacated spot.

The high post man who can remember to look for the open cut to the goal after he passes the ball to a side or corner can pick up a lot of easy points over the season. If the low post has cut to the area under the goal already, the high post can stay up or, better yet, cut to the spot under the goal opposite the low post to get in good rebound position. As a team the post men will always try to stay opposite each other whether that be high and low or on the right and left sides of the lane.

Post men should learn to mix their timing up when they cut to the ball and when they cut around the goal area when the ball is on the side or in the corner. I prefer that the posts hold their position momentarily as the ball is passed around the outside and then cut quickly and decisively when they do decide to cut to the ball. Post men who just wander around all night in the interior seldom get good openings. A good example of this is shown in diagram 2-19. Player 5 will not be open inside if he floats aimlessly down toward the baseline as the ball is passed from 2 to 4. If 5 hesitates a half-count and then rolls down hard to the base, he may be able to beat the defender. Player 3's cut complements 5's roll. This post roll-down move is a strong one against defenses that match up well inside. It is especially a good ploy from the 1-3-1 set. (See drills.)

Last here, but not in order of importance, is to emphasize

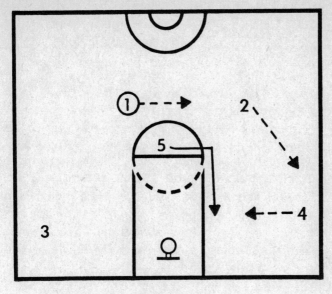

Diagram 2-19

daily to the inside people their tremendous rebounding assignment. The best penetration of all is the offensive rebound. Since
the defense will have a tougher job blocking out the offense in
many cases, the post men can fulfill their rebounding roles more
easily than against the man-to-man oftentimes. But they have to
be cognizant of the value of the rebound game and will have to
want to get the job done. The posts will be wise to try to keep
from being on the same rebound side often and must remember
that most rebounds go to the side opposite the shot. Even if the
post players are not tall, they can do a good job of hurting the
zone overall if they will focus in on these various responsibilities.

Specific Techniques for Wing or Corner Play

The wings must follow the principle established in the first
chapter of keeping generally wide so that the interior can be
open for penetration through cuts and passes to the post. While

there may be special plays set up which call for the wings to move in to screen or cut, the general plan should be for the wings to help keep the offense in motion with the guards. In line with that responsibility, the wings must know the job of the point man or the guards because the wings are so often rotated into the front spots. Even from the wing or corner positions, however, the wings have a responsibility to help the guards with penetration and with keeping the offense moving. They must be alert to adjust to the appropriate spots when there is a punch, cut, pull, or rotate initiated by a guard. In addition, the wings may themselves initiate any one of these motion-producing moves. When the wings feel the offense is in a stymie, they can cut. When there is a gap, they can punch into it. In other words, all of the periphery players have much the same responsibilities, even though the guards bear a greater burden than the wings when it comes to setting plays.

The wings must remember to observe the movement of the posts so that when a post decides to rotate to a spot vacated on a pull or rotate move, the wing moves to the corner area. Anytime the high post gets the ball, the wings should remember to head for the corner area and read the defense for openings.

Also, I like to have any man who has been rotated into a corner to rove the baseline when the ball is reversed. This move fits into so many nice plays that we use. In diagram 2-20, player 2 rotated to the corner and in the reversal cut opposite. The posts execute a cross move on the flow back. A cut on the baseline or even into the foul line in some situations is a much stronger move than having the man simply float back up into the wing area or just stay standing in the corner.

Again, it is well to remind the wing player of his responsibility in the rebounding game. At least one of the wings will be in on the inside rebounding battle each time, while the other is either in the long rebound position or in defensive balance, since he will probably be one of the guards.

We are now ready to put together the team principles and the various pointers for individual execution and set up some basic moves that can be used spontaneously or in various sequences to effect the Organized Free-Lance system.

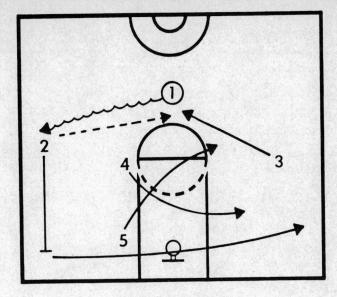

Diagram 2-20

Suggestions for Individuals in Zone Offensive Play

1. When you cut, do it quickly and surely. Don't float.

2. When you get the ball, assume a triple threat position. Be ready to drive, shoot, or pass inside.

3. Have your inside foot set when anticipating a pass on the perimeter. When you get the ball, square around and look at the goal. Hold for a two-count when possible in order to give cutters a chance to move, especially with the ball on the sides. Try not to hold more than a three-count, however.

4. Look for the drive.

5. Inside men must pull out one step in the direction opposite of every drive toward the goal.

6. Bounce pass inside.

7. When the defense gets matched up, initiate a cut or dribble move.

8. Punch if you see a gap. You are the boss with the ball.

9. If you do not have the ball, stay wide on the wing or deep at the point, or cut to an open hole.

10. Keep up movement on the inside. Never stand still inside the offense.

11. Use dribble-pulls to help set up inside passes. Break the three-in-a-row line.

12. Move up and down in the posts. Stay very active in the posts and be ready to come as far out as 25 feet in order to get open in the middle.

13. Pass to the high post whenever you can.

14. The high post man must always turn and look under, then opposite, when he gets the ball.

15. Posts must time their rolls and cuts. Do not drift.

3

Organizing the Free-Lance Zone Offense System

While the first two chapters give meaning to this one, this chapter also serves to tie together the theory of the first chapter and the technique of the second. Chapter One served to tell the "why" and Chapter Two told the "how." This one will show "what" to do with the previous material. The chapters subsequent to this will further expand on specific applications against the various zone styles.

After many years of experimenting with various offenses, I have developed a core group of zone moves that I call the Basic Five. This indicates the five basic

free-lance moves I want my players to learn to attack the zone
defenses, and they may be used from any starting formation.
Although I will discuss each individually, briefly the description
of the five moves is: "Punch it, Dribble it, Cut it, High-low it,
and Screen it!" The foregoing sentence is the one I use in de-
scribing to players in quick fashion their free-lance zone options.
They may use any of these options in a spontaneous manner in
any order they desire, depending on their judgment as to what is
called for in a specific situation. Once they realize that the defense is containing, laning, or matching, they will be able to
react with moves that can give the best offensive advantage. As
noted earlier, however, if the players cannot get the desired
attack on their own, there are set plays which use these moves in
sequence that the coach can call into play. If a team can perform
each of the Basic Five moves, it can execute nearly every zone
offense it will be asked to learn in very little time. They are an
attack of their own when used in free-lance. But they form the
fundamental nucleus for most effective zone plays, as well.

The Basic Five

Punch it! The most fundamental of the Basic Five is the
punch move because it can be employed against any zone that
makes the mistake of allowing a gap to appear in its defense of
the ballhandler. Since we have discussed the move fully in the
first two chapters, a few diagrams will suffice to illustrate the
regular punch and the one-on-one punch. Diagram 3-1 shows
the punch by 1 from a 2-3 offense against a 1-2-2. Seeing the gap,
1 bounces until the defense flexes. Just before he encounters
heavy pressure, he picks up the dribble and looks to feed 3, who
stepped up, 2, who flared, or 5, who also stepped up. In diagram
3-2 player 3 punches against the same 1-2-2. He may have faked
his defense to the corner first to help open the gap, or he could
have used the dribble-spin move into his defender to get there.
This is an excellent use of that valuable offensive weapon. Regardless, once in the gap he looks to feed 5, who pulls, or to

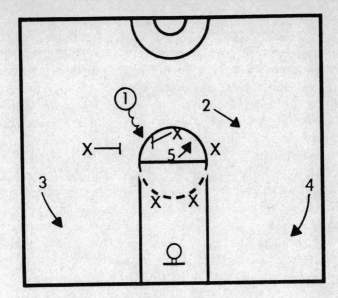

Diagram 3-1

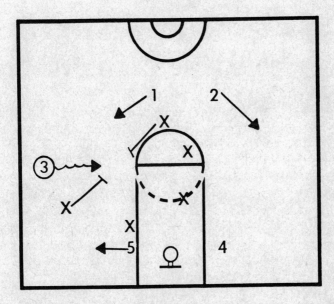

Diagram 3-2

either of the guards who have made their corresponding moves. If nothing materializes, the play continues, and the offense will search for a new move to employ.

In diagram 3-3 point 1 uses a one-on-one punch move that can be used often by a clever guard. Even though there is no defensive gap, often the point man can take the man defending him right into a wing defender. It takes a good defender on the ballhandler to prevent this move from happening. As the ballhandler angles right at the wing defender, the offensive wing player flares quickly two or three steps. If the wing defender is influenced by the point man to come toward the ball, 3 has an easy opening. If the man on 5 comes to cover 3, the inside is in jeopardy.

Diagram 3-4 shows one of my favorite moves against all zones and will work against the man-to-man, too. (Not that it works *every* time, but it forces the defense to make a quick adjustment or else yield a good shot.) The wing punch is made by 2 as he punches toward the baseline. If he gets through his defender, he can continue, of course, but the move is simply to punch toward the goal on the base to get the defender on 5 to flex down. Post man 5 pops out one or two steps as the punch is made and looks for the quick pass from 2. Player 1 gives deep outlet support in order to prevent offensive stagnation and to allow for the reversal. (See drills.)

The punch move is most effective against the laning zones, but will be effective for all zone variations. Players must remember the technique of jabbing back out after they have punched in and passed off. Drilling the punch moves with three-on-three and even five-on-five and emphasizing its importance will help the players to become masters of this valuable move.

Dribble it! Any of the peripheral players may initiate one of the three lateral dribble moves at any time in order to help set up the passing game and to break up defensive stymies. While more effective against the containing and matchup styles, they can be used against the laning zones as well, especially the dribble-pull. The three lateral dribble moves (punching and

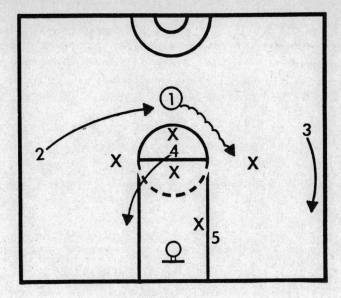

Diagram 3-3

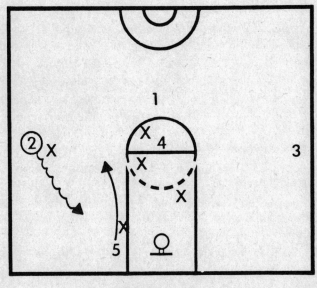

Diagram 3-4

driving are vertical dribble moves) are the dribble-rotate, the dribble-pull, and the dribble-up. Each move is calculated to help set up either penetrating or peripheral passing.

Diagram 3-5 shows a guard dribble-rotate move from a 2-1-2 set. The points of technique in execution will be recalled from Chapter Two. Player 2 dribbles wide quickly to the wing spot. Wing 4 slides to the corner and waits until the ball is reversed to cut hard on the baseline to the other side. Post 5 times his cut to roll down to the goal just after 2 has come to a stop. If he cuts too soon, 2 cannot feed him. By waiting he gives 2 a chance to pass quickly to 4 in the corner who can really feed nicely to 5 if he puts a good move on the man covering the post. If nothing works after the reversal, the offense will try another move. Note that the defense was matched to the offense. If the offense was stagnant or if pressure from laning the wings had slowed down the movement, this exercise will get the ball to the side, force some defensive adjustment, and give an opportunity for the post man to beat his man. Of course player 4 can initiate a dribble to the corner move if 2 does not perform the dribble to the wing. The play would then continue the same way, with 5 rolling down and 4 going opposite after reversing the ball.

In diagram 3-6 the dribble-pull is used from a 1-4 set. This move is a terrific point offense exercise. The post opposite the dribble-pull knows that when the point guard bounces laterally and picks up the ball that he should pop out quickly (we call this "pop the post") and look for the pass. He should go as high as he must in order to get open because we want him to get the basketball. When he gets it, 5 cuts across the lane to get free and the wings both drop to the corner. The wings are caught in between, having to cover 1 and 3 on the right side in this 1-3-1 defense and having to choose between 4 and 2 on the left. The low post is occupied with 5's cut. The high post defender almost has to come high to cover the ball in 4's hands because if the wing on the left does so, 2 is clearly open. This means that 5 is in a one-on-one situation down low and this is certainly good for the offense. If 4 feeds a wing, he cuts to the goal. If he drops it back off to 1 who slides opposite his pass to the post, he can cut right back into the post again.

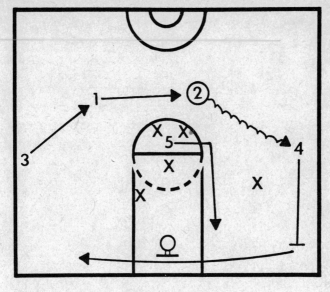

Diagram 3-5

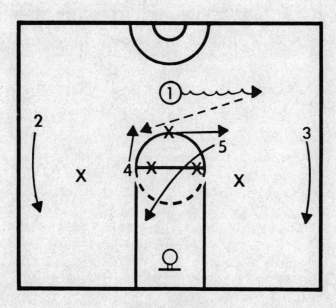

Diagram 3-6

This move is effective against point defenses, but is not as effective against two-front defenses. Common sense will show why it is not as good against a 2-3, for example. The players start in gap positions to the 2-3 by lining up in a 1-4. The cuts in popping the post move the offense right into the 2-3 positions. Thus, coaches must think before calling out certain plays. This is why it is hard to imagine how any one offense could go against every style of zone defense. This exercise in diagram 3-6 is so successful against a point defense, whether it is matching, laning, or containing. But if the opponent changes to a two-front conventional zone, the offense will have to use other of the 1-4 options in order to get free.

Diagram 3-7 pictures a dribble-up move from the corner, the best place to use it. Against a 1-3-1 the ball is passed from 2 to 5 in the corner. Wing 2 cuts toward the goal and pivots to look back to 5. If 5 should reverse the pass to 1 coming over, 2 would just go on through. This move is called a corner-slide and will be discussed in the section on cutting. If, however, player 5 drib-

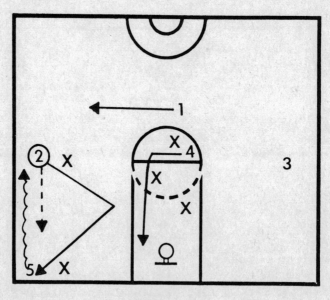

Diagram 3-7

bles up to the wing, this is 2's key that the dribble-up is being used and he cuts right to the corner area where the defensive man is trying to decide whether or not to go on up with 5 as he dribbles out. Post 4 then times his cut in order to try to beat his man to the goal. If nothing happens yet, on the reversal the point man will have to work on both 1 and 3 if the passes are quick. The dribble-up is the least used of the lateral dribble moves but can be very effective against the 1-3-1, 1-2-2 and matchups.

Cut it. The first kind of cutting is the kind that is hard to put into a diagram because it involves the individual cut to the open spot as it develops between himself and the ballhandler. It is this kind of free-lance cutting that will make our system and any other system more effective. I have referred to the unpredictable nature of zone defense before. You can never be sure just where you will find players in a zone defense, regardless of the style or formation. Zone players seem to float around more. In planning for offensive strategy against the man-to-man, you can place players around the court and be sure that the defense will be somewhere in close proximity to the offense and you can plan your cuts and screens to match the defense. But against the zones, you may find the defenders almost anywhere. Usually, if the offense will handle the ball skillfully and with patience, the defense will stretch in places and allow a hole to appear. Players in every position, inside and out, must be reminded constantly in the early practices to watch for these openings between themselves and the ball. And everyone must remember the principle of moving on out of the hole if he fails to get the ball in order to keep the middle open and to keep the offense in motion. A player who cuts to the open spot must circle cut or V-cut back out or continue on through the defense to the opposite side from which he came. A spread offense that has a lot of action in the posts will be able to have this kind of cutting game most consistently. The best way to teach it is to have a half-court game of five or ten minutes occasionally in which the only way a man can shoot is if he gets the ball on a pass after he has cut into a hole in the defense. Later, this game may be expanded to include one other of the Basic Five moves, if desired. I have found it to be difficult to teach players to read holes in the defense in any other way. Three man drills do not seem to accommodate this technique like five-on-five.

There are other effective cuts against zones besides the cut to the hole. You will recall the high post give and go move from our earlier discussion. We want to make this an automatic response by the post man as the season progresses. Of course, this can be drilled nicely in three or four man exercises. (See drills.) Further, any peripheral player can use the give and go at any time he desires in the Organized Free-Lance system. As the ballhandler realizes the offense is getting stagnant or well-covered by the defense, he may stir up the offense by initiating a give and go. It's also good against tight ball pressure. To give and go will create offensive motion and defensive adjustment. If the players on the periphery will rotate toward the ball when a man cuts for the goal, someone may get open in the spot vacated by the cutter. If not, the reverse passing game will be enhanced by all outside players rotating rapidly over one offensive spot toward the ball. Simply rotate one slot as 2 does in diagram 3-8 and as 2 and 4 do in diagram 3-9.

Of special interest is the give and go when executed by the wing man. This move was one of the first popular zone offense exercises and continues to be used by many coaches today. It is as fundamental to zone play as the split the post or the screen and roll are to man-to-man. So, we call this particular move the "corner slide down" move, and our players may employ it any time from almost any formation. (See drills.) Diagram 3-10 shows it from the 1-3-1 set with 2 using the give and go with 5 in the corner. Post man 4 times his cut to get into the area near the goal just after 2 clears through. Any time the wing passes to the corner, he will do well to use the give and go. The 1-2-2 and the 1-4 adapt quite well to this, and we will deal with them in a later chapter on this move.

Screen it! In the discussion of screening in Chapter Two I found it necessary to diagram the basic screening moves in order to clarify what was being discussed regarding the techniques of

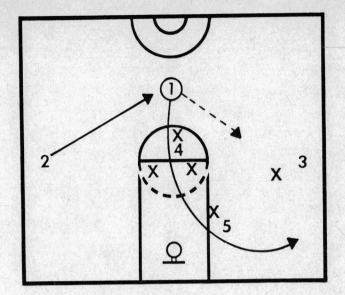

Diagram 3-8

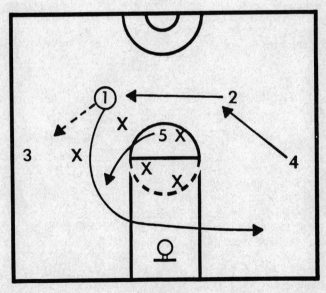

Diagram 3-9

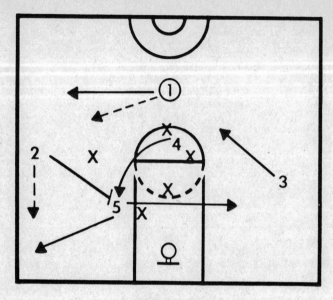

Diagram 3-10

zone screening. One should turn to those pages to see where screening may be done most effectively, but as a simple reminder for our purposes here, I will reiterate that the basic screening exercises against the zones are the post screen for the point, the post screen for the other post, the baseline screens, the weakside two-man game screens, and the baseline man screen the wing. All of these moves may be broken down into three man drills, although a team need not employ all of these in order to be effective. (See drills.) With the exception of the baseline series of screens, the rest of the screens can be set up spontaneously as the screener sees the opportunity arise. For example, the high post man can easily come out and offer the point man a screen on his own at any time. No signal need be given. It is just like the other Basic Five moves we have discussed previously. When there is an appropriate occasion, the opportunistic player utilizes one of his offensive tools. I have found that teaching screening against the zones has helped us tremendously because many of the set plays we use involve some screening. There is a valuable carryover once the players have the knowledge of screening techniques. And screening has a place against all styles of zones, which makes an additional plus.

High-low it! Again, the single most important area of attack is the post area. Even in a single-post alignment, there will still be general high and low post responsibility as the ball is passed around the floor. The post responsibilities are clear in the 1-3-1, 1-2-2 and the 1-4. But even in the 2-1-2, when the ball is on a side, the player in the opposite wing area is responsible to penetrate the low post area if a pass goes into the high post, for example.

The coach must acquaint every player, who may be playing much time at all in the post areas, of their responsibility to create continuous inside movement. Although I have mentioned the various possible moves for the inside people earlier, it is worthwhile to re-emphasize in a combined statement the nature of the inside game. *First,* the posts work as a team. They watch each other and talk together. They avoid getting too close together so that one man can defend them both, except at the exact moment of a screen, of course. They must change positions in a double post offense at least every three passes. Standing or laterally moving post men are too easy to guard.

Second, the man in the high post must go as high out on the floor as necessary to get open. He has to get open often if every third or fourth pass is to go into the post area in an effective offense. The high-low post passes and the pop the post move of the Basic Five will wreck zone defenses more than any other single move. (So much so, in fact, that I would almost say that the rest of the offensive moves are actually alternative moves in between attempts to get post action.)

Third, the high post player should time his cuts and rolls toward the goal or ball, rather than drift around in the general area of the goal as so many post men do. The post players must cut, spin and fight to get open. They must really work hard to execute a freeing move inside, because the offense must get the ball in there often and the defense knows that it can not permit it to happen. The real war in a game takes place inside. Everyone must be prepared.

Fourth, when a post man passes out of the middle to a wing, he must not stand back to see how things go. He must cut right into the rebound game and look for a return pass while he does.

Fifth, if a driver is coming into the area occupied by a post man, he must pull out opposite the driver to give room for the drive and to look for a drop-off pass to himself. As mentioned before, practice on this one move can really pay dividends against all kinds of defenses.

Sixth, the posts should screen for each other after three passes or cut in a circle from low post to high and vice-versa. Or when the posts are on the same side of the ball (as in diagram 3-11), and the ball is reversed, the posts should cross, form an "X," as they change high and low positions on the movement of the ball. This exercise causes the defense to have to do much more adjusting than any other method of movement. Several plays from the 1-3-1, 1-2-2 and 1-4 can utilize crossing the posts.

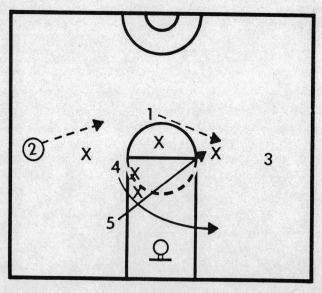

Diagram 3-11

And the last point is to be sure to stress and to practice the rebound game. Rugged board play will cover up for almost any other deficiency in the game. Rebounding can make a high scoring team out of an outfit that is unable to do a lot of points of execution very well.

In summary on post play, when we yell out that we want to high-low it, we mean we want our post people to get more active and we want our outside players to perform all the moves possible to help create more high and low post play. When we are not getting the ball into the posts enough, the scoreboard will remind us. If we had only one play, it would be to pass the ball to the high post then cut the wings toward the baseline while sliding the guards to the wing areas. If the post will turn and look under, then opposite, a lot will happen.

The coach can help his teaching load by compiling lists of things each player should know about the system and about his position in particular and give them to the players to memorize. It is important that the players have a general concept of why they are doing various things and how their role fits into the whole thing that the team is trying to accomplish. Along with the knowledge of whether the defense is laning, containing, or matching up, the Organized Free-Lance system forms a workable and compact attack against the various zone styles. The combination of exercises allows the offensive players a variety of moves calculated to give the offense adequate opportunities for the three things it has to have to win—ball movement, player movement, and penetration. From these same moves, by placing two or three in a set combination, the coach can form hundreds of patterns or set plays without having to worry about teaching new techniques. After some good practices, the players will react to the possibilities quickly as they present themselves in scrimmage. Still, the process of refinement will be a season-long process as in any offense. The players will grow in the offense. They should enjoy the challenge of learning five moves that they will be able to use on their own to beat the opponent's zone. Hopefully, they will look forward to seeing the zone instead of dreading it as many teams do.

4

Attacking Containing
Zones with the Basic Five

In the previous chapters I
have presented the philosophy of
zone offense that I believe to be
most effective along with a core set
of moves called the Basic Five
which serve as the basis for our Organized Free-Lance system as well
as for the special set patterns or
plays that we use in particular situations against various zone defenses.
The intention of the entire system is
to enable the players to have as
much variation as possible in attacking zones without having to learn
too many different and unrelated offenses.

In the next four chapters we

will discuss how to use the Basic Five against the containing, matching, and laning defenses. In addition, I will present some patterns which borrow from the Basic Five that can be used against these defensive variations when the offense is not functioning satisfactorily on a free-lance basis.

You will remember that we will allow our team to have first crack at the defense by using the Basic Five from whatever formation in which we desire to begin. We used to attack an even-numbered defensive front with a point or odd-numbered front in order to begin in the gaps. However, this is not totally necessary. A team may begin with the same formation against every zone, keeping in mind that against one set of defenses it is beginning in the gaps and in the other it is beginning matched with the defensive front. Nowadays with so many teams using some matchup principles, it is just as likely that the defensive front will adjust to match the offensive alignment, anyway. As a result, it matters little how the offense begins. It is more important how the players respond when they see a gap, or see they are matched up, or see the defense begin to jump out into the pass lanes. Therefore in this and the following chapter, we will discuss the point and two-front attacks interchangeably, against both even and odd defensive frontals.

Playing Against the 2-3 with the Basic Five

It would be difficult to show all the possible combinations that can be used from the Basic Five. For example, there are 25 combinations with which any two of the individual moves could be used from any particular starting alignment. Then there are various ways that techniques like cutting or dribble moves can be used, not to mention the fact that the Basic Five can be run from any formation. Then, if a team has the patience to use three moves in any order before shooting, the possible combination of available moves rises into the hundreds. This emphasizes the whole point, that knowing five moves and having an idea when to utilize each will give a team all the attack it needs against a zone. The following diagrams will help get the reader's mind attuned to the system by showing some of these possibilities. Each coach can add combinations to the listing as he sees fit.

Punching. Diagram 4-1 shows the many punch routes that a 1-3-1 offense would have if the 2-3 zone did not adjust to match up with the offense. Naturally, not all of these would be open at

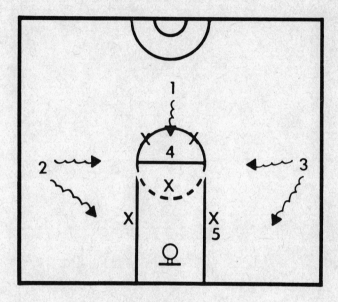

Diagram 4-1

the same time, but these spots are where men in the various positions should look for holes to punch. In diagram 4-2 the 2-1-2 can look for gaps to appear in front of them as shown if the 1-3-1 or 1-2-2 does not seal up properly. For specific moves with punching the containing defenses, the reader may refer to Chapters Two and Three where we discussed punching. We will spend more time with punching when we deal with lane zones, since it comes up much more frequently against that style than against the containing.

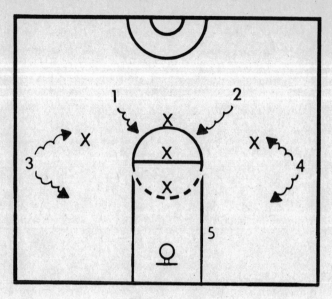

Diagram 4-2

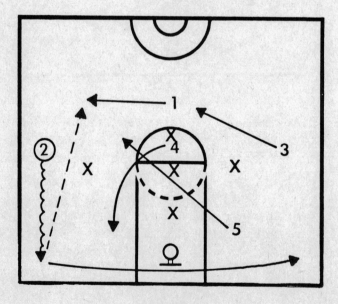

Diagram 4-3

Using lateral dribble moves. Diagram 4-3 illustrates a dribble-rotate from a 1-3-1 against a 1-3-1 or when another defensive formation has moved to matching positions against a 1-3-1 offense. Wing player 2 dribbles to the corner and the periphery players rotate behind him. The posts circle. On the reversal, if there is one, 2 will rove the base and the posts will cross. The diagrams in Chapters Two and Three offer different examples in which the front men initiate the rotations. In diagram 4-4 wing man 5 starts the dribble rotate from a 1-4 set against a 1-2-2. The moves for the offensive players are the same as in the preceeding example.

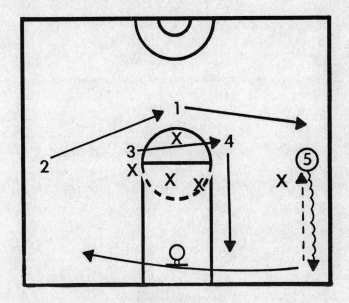

Diagram 4-4

The dribble-pull from a 1-4 formation appears in diagram 4-5. Post man 5 comes up on the pop the post move against a 1-3-1. Post 4 crosses in front of the goal as 5 turns and faces the goal, while the wings drop to the corners. In diagram 4-6 the defense is 2-3 or has matched up to a 2-1-2 offense. Guard 1 pulls his defender two steps over and post 5 pops up to break the

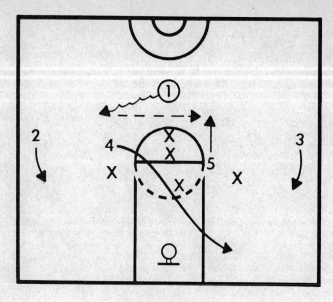

Diagram 4-5

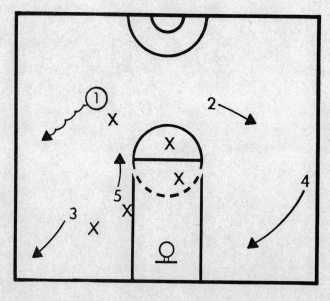

Diagram 4-6

three-in-a-row situation he was in with 1 and the defender on 1. As 5 gets the ball, he turns and looks under to 4 and opposite to 2 for openings. Continuing with yet another pull from a different position, diagram 4-7 shows wing 3 pulling a couple of bounces to set up his pass into the post areas. Note that they each adjust to the pull as prescribed earlier in Chapter Three. If 3 cannot pass inside, he can still pass to 1 who may find himself or 2 in a gap.

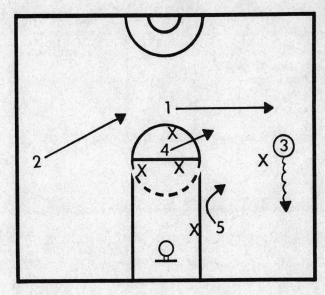

Diagram 4-7

Cutting the zone. Guard and forward cuts are shown in diagram 4-8 from a 1-4. Point 1 passes to 2 and cuts through the 1-2-2 to the ballside corner. Wing 3 fills in for 1. If 2 passes to 1 in the corner, he can cut across in a corner slide move. Posts 4 and 5 move accordingly and can cross on the reversal of the ball.

In diagram 4-9 guard 2 felt he saw an opening behind the defense and cut to it. Being closed off by the off-side back man, he made a "V" cut back out to the corner vacated by 4. However, before cutting up to the front, 4 looked for a cross-court

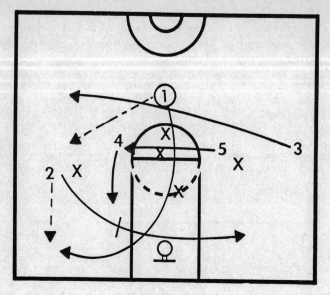

Diagram 4-8

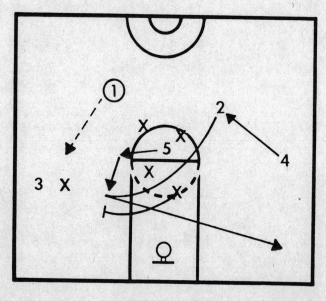

Diagram 4-9

pass from 3. Of course this doesn't look like much of a move because 2 did not get open, but it demonstrates how 2 could cut and how 4 and 5 then read to try to get free. Regardless, it is still their ball and they are free to use a new option.

Diagram 4-10 shows another off-side cut to the ball. This time wing 3 continues on through the defense when he fails to get open on his initial cut. Continuing with the same series in diagram 4-11, 2 passes to 3 and cuts across on a corner slide. Posts 4 and 5 cross on the reversal as player 1 must pull the ball over a bit to get a good passing lane to the weak side. It is just this kind of occasion in which a fake reversal and a quick pass right back to 3 in the corner area may work. Cutting and movement such as this will cause the defense to have to adjust a lot. The coach should be sure that the team does not do so much cutting that the ball is slowed down too much, however. There are times to increase the amount of cutting and there are times to decrease it. The coach must be evaluating the efficacy of what is happening on the court at all times.

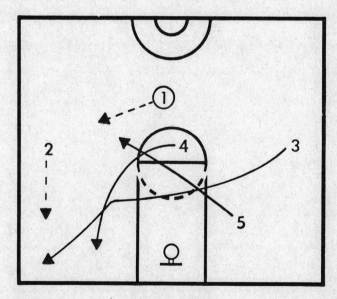

Diagram 4-10

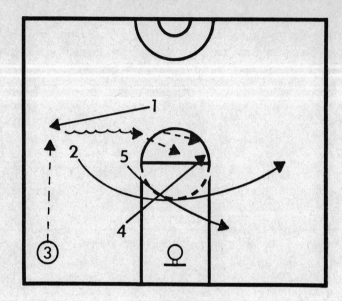

Diagram 4-11

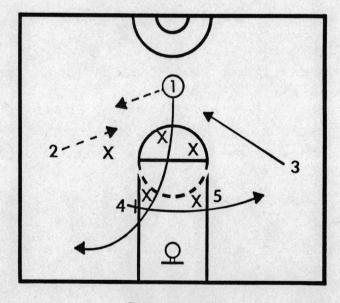

Diagram 4-12

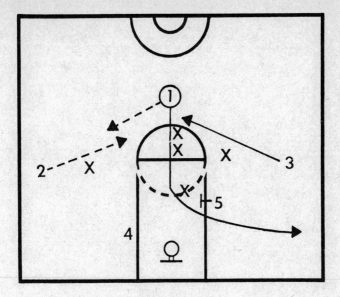

Diagram 4-13

Screening the zone. In addition to the examples of screening in the previous two chapters, consider the moves in diagram 4-12 and 4-13. Point 1 starts in a 1-2-2 offense and comes under post 4 in the first diagram. On the reversal of the ball, 4 comes out from under 5's screen. Remember from our discussion of screening technique that the screeners are as likely to be open as the cutters. In diagram 4-13 point 1 decides to cut opposite and use 5's screen. The reverse action would be like the preceeding picture in that 5 would cut off of 4's screen as the ball goes by 2.

Using the high and low posts. Keep in mind the importance that the coach must place on the high and low post movement as discussed in Chapter Three. Diagrams 4-14 through 4-16 show some more examples of high and low action. In diagram 4-14, 4 breaks out high on his own to get open. Remembering that he should throw the ball to a post man *anytime he can get him the ball* and at least every third or fourth pass, 1 feeds him high and slides away from him in order to get himself free. Low post 5

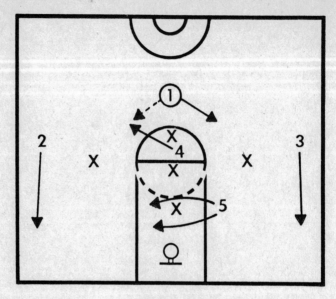

Diagram 4-14

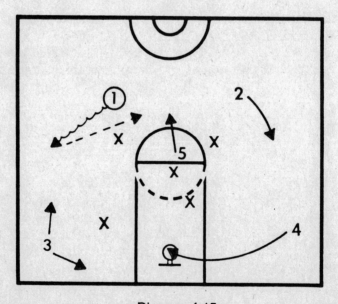

Diagram 4-15

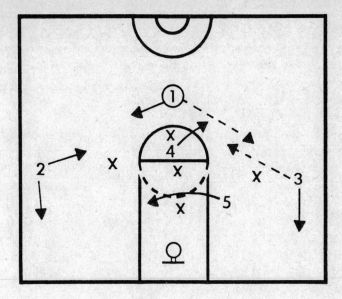

Diagram 4-16

remembers his rule to cross under as 4 faces the goal and the wings make their prescribed move to the corner areas, reading for openings. In diagram 4-15 guard 1 pulls to get 5 up out of the post in a 2-1-2 lineup that has been matched up by the defensive shifting. As 5 gets the ball and faces up, he looks under for 4 and opposite for 2 who reads for an opening, depending on how the front defender reacts to the fact that 5 now has the ball. In the last of the three pictures, wing 3 feeds 4 who has stepped high on his own to help free himself. Again, the players respond by crossing underneath and flaring on the side opposite the pass. Player 3 can help himself by reading the reactions of the man who was defending both him and 5 in order to try to get open himself.

It is not feasible to show all the various possibilities in diagrams in each chapter, so I will try to space out as many of them as we proceed in the book and to avoid further repetition whenever it is possible. As one can see, the importance of the starting formation in offense and defense is not quite as important as is often imagined unless the defense fails to move at all. If that be the case, it will be easy to beat that kind of defense, anyway. Thus, since most good defenses will adjust to the movements of the offense and the ball, it is more important for the offensive players to be able to see a hole when it opens and to know how to deal with it. It is important to realize when the defense has caught up with the offense into more or less matched alignment and to create movement through cuts, dribble moves, or inside motion.

Changing the starting formation for the offense will cause the defense to have to adjust to it for a time or two down the floor, but eventually the defense will be right with the offense again unless the players are good at reading the defense. This is why we emphasize the need for players to have an offensive style that can adjust to the demands placed on it by the defense. I believe the educated reading of a defense as to its containing, matching, or laning techniques, complemented with a free-lance style, is best for playing against the unpredictable nature of zone defenses.

Special Moves Against All Zone Styles

There are two special moves we employ against the changing styles of zones that can be classified as plays. I am putting them in a separate spot here because these moves do not correlate with the Basic Five quite as readily as all the rest of the moves that we will discuss as we proceed. The two plays are called the Corner Game and the Hook and Rub Game.

Corner Game. All of the zone defenses are in the same 2-3 position when the ball is in the corner of the offense. A device which tends to give more predictability to a zone is to move the ball into the corner and know that the offense is going to have to face a 2-3 from that position. An advantage for the good one-on-one team is that it enhances the opportunity for man-to-man kind of offensive play. A disadvantage for poor ballhandlers or poor reactors is that the ball can get stuck in the corner by trapping and laning techniques. Diagram 4-17 shows the setup

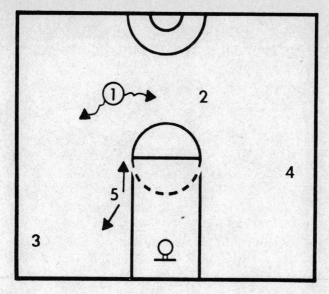

Diagram 4-17

of the Corner Game. Players 1, 3, and 5 form a triangle while 2 and 4 are in position for a quick reversal man-to-man game. Player 1 has to be the playmaker and must use the dribble-pull technique frequently in order to move the ball to the post and corner. The ball may be released to 2 at any time and he may pass back to 1 who will try to penetrate with the triangle again, or 2 and 4 can run a weakside two-man game against the two weakside defenders who have to be in a man-to-man situation, as in diagram 4-18. The offense can be used from the new side either by sliding 5 over to the new post position and using 4 as the corner man or by letting 3 rove the base as in diagram 4-19. Player 4 may then play the post or can change with 5 and become the opposite side forward again. The offense may change sides of the floor also by using the dribble as shown in diagram 4-20, with 3 roving the base and 4 and 5 changing positions in the event 5 is the only legitimate inside player. If 1 is the only real playmaker or else cannot shoot well, he and 2 can rotate spots to keep 1 in the feeding position. (See pp. 98-99).

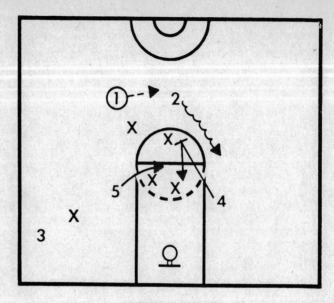

Diagram 4-18

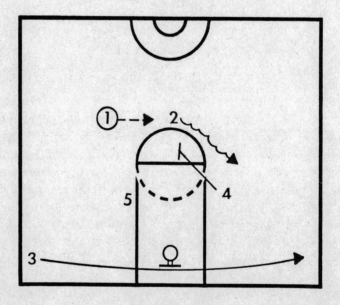

Diagram 4-19

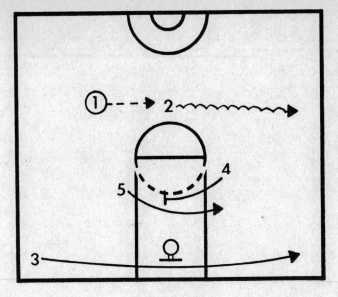

Diagram 4-20

The Corner Game sets up a two-man game and is good for setting up a one-on-one inside game for the team that has a capable post man. Since every zone has to fall to 2-3 with the ball on the side, it lets the offense know from where to expect the defense to come. Also, since it is often the inferior team who is hoping to equalize the difference in the teams by using the zone, the man-to-man aspects of this move are very appealing to the offensive team in many cases.

The Hook and Rub Game. While this move may be a little less effective against the lane zones, it will be generally effective against all styles. In diagram 4-21 the offense is starting from a 2-3 set against a 2-3 or a defense that has become matched through adjustment. Guard 1 passes to 3 and cuts to a spot where he can position up and get the ball. If he cannot, 5 pops out high and gets the ball from 3, who cuts, rubbing right in front of 1. Player 1 then hooks right out toward the wing and the ball. Post 5 tries to feed 1 or 3. If he cannot he reverses the ball

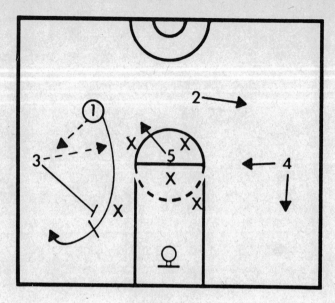

Diagram 4-21

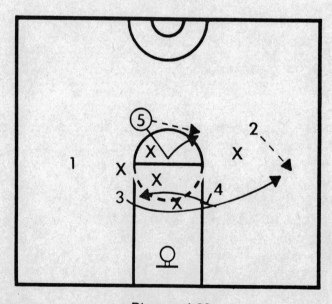

Diagram 4-22

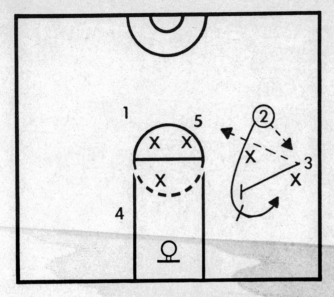

Diagram 4-23

to 2 (which he could have done sooner, had he so desired). Diagram 4-22 shows the reverse action as 3 comes off of 4, who screens and looks. In diagram 4-23, we see the completion as 2 and 3 run the hook and rub on the opposite side of the floor. Note that 1 and 5 have moved to their home spots. This move gives opportunities for penetration and for short range shots and has good rebounding.

In diagram 4-24 the same move is used from the 1-3-1 offensive formation against a 1-2-2. All the moves are the same as diagram 4-25 shows the beginning of the reverse play. (See p. 102.)

If the coach does not want to work on the reverse part of the game, the team can still benefit from the hook and rub on the first side, and then if the play fails to produce a shot, the offense can realign and run something else.

In the early part of the season the players will experience more difficulty recognizing items like the gaps, the holes, when a team is laning, or when the offense is being made stagnant by good adjustment and little movement. Therefore, the coach may

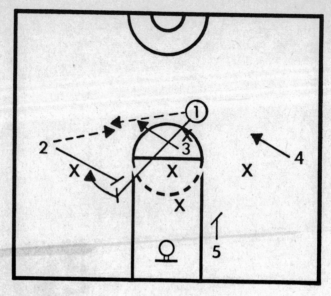

Diagram 4-24

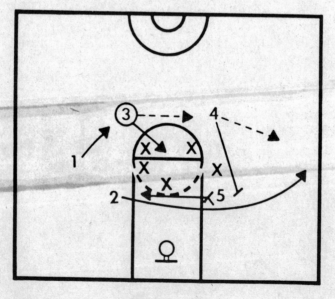

Diagram 4-25

have to call time out after a few minutes and explain what they
need to do more of—cutting, high-low post passing, dribble-
rotations, or whatever. Soon, he may have to call for a set play
which he thinks will fit the defense at the time. It is gratifying,
however, as the season progresses to have a team be able to stay
on its own longer against a zone with only a little help from the
coach as to what free-lance move it should be using more. Eventually, if the team is able to drive an opponent out of its zone
completely on its own, it is indeed a fine evening. In the next
chapter we will discuss some plays that may be used against the
various containing zones that call upon the Basic Five moves,
but in a set order.

5

Utilizing Zone Offense Plays
Against the Containing Zones

This chapter illustrates some special moves to be used against the containing zones that incorporate the same moves learned in the Basic Five. It would be interesting for each coach to look at the diagrams of the plays he used last year against zones. In most cases, I would guess, his patterns used exercises that are Basic Five moves. Naturally, no single team would use all of the plays listed in this and the succeeding chapters. I suggest that the Basic Five be learned and that you then add three or four special zone plays. I would recommend that each team know two plays which go against containing zones and one each for the matchups and the laning types. This is relative to the frequency with which a team faces these defenses.

Baseline Pinch

In the earlier chapters we have noted some various moves using baseline screens. This Baseline Pinch move is effective against any containing lineup, but the screens must be executed as described in Chapters Two and Three. Diagram 5-1 shows the 2-3 alignment with 1 passing to 3 and changing with 2, which is optional. Wing 3 looks in at 5 and can use free-lance moves of driving, punching, or pulling. If three reverses the ball, 4

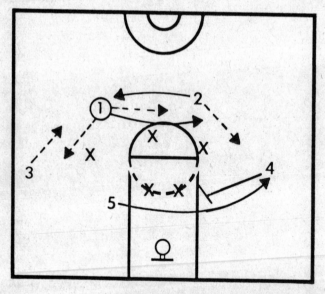

Diagram 5-1

pinches in on the baseline, and 5 cuts to the wing. Diagram 5-2 shows the continuation if 5 or 4 are not open in the initial diagram. The offense continues with a series of baseline pinches while the guards may change with each other at will, looking for

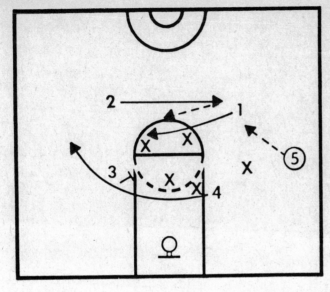

Diagram 5-2

opportunities to punch or pass inside. In this and all of the plays we will discuss, when one of the players sees a really good free-lance opening to cut, drive, punch, or use another appropriate free-lance move, then by all means he should do it.

Box and Floater

In diagram 5-3 we have a 2-2 formation with a quality forward 4, playing on the stack with 5. The floater is 4, and he can go to any of the three positions shown in diagrams 5-3 through 5-5. If the ball goes opposite, as in diagram 5-3, 4 can cut into any opening he reads in the middle, and then 5 reads how the defense reacts to 4's move. If there is no play, 4 and 5 readjust. In diagram 5-4, 4 has broken out to the wing to get the basketball. In this case 3 and 5 read the inside defense. Keep in mind that the free-lance options are open in every movement of the ball. Floater 4 breaks high to get open from the guard in diagram

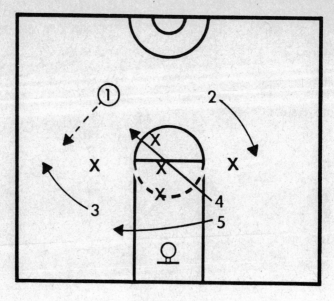

Diagram 5-3

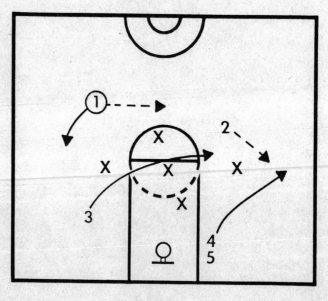

Diagram 5-4

5-5 and then turns to feed under or opposite. In this move the slide of player 2 is very significant. This offense is quite simple and borrows heavily from the free-lance knowledge of the players, but with a good basketball player at the 4 position, it is quite an effective offense against all containing formations.

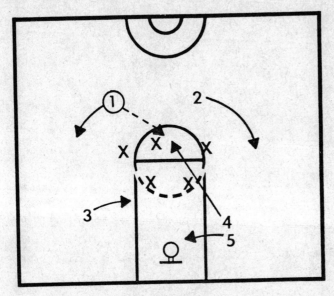

Diagram 5-5

The 2-2-1 Screener

This is an effective offense against the 1-3-1 and 1-2-2 lineups, utilizing a good variety of screening options. In diagram 5-6, guard 2 initiates a screen for 1, who then drives off of him, looking for a shot. If he cannot shoot or play quickly with 2, he feeds 4, who can play or pass to 3 coming off of 5's screen. If 5 makes a good screen and look back move, he may be open. This offense can continue as a continuity by having 4 cut across to the opposite wing after passing to either 3 or 1. The original setup is then recreated. In diagram 5-7, 5 exercises one of his options of

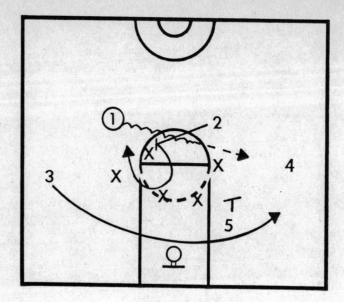

Diagram 5-6

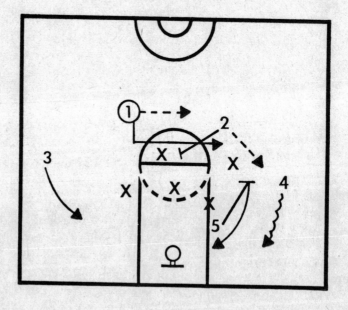

Diagram 5-7

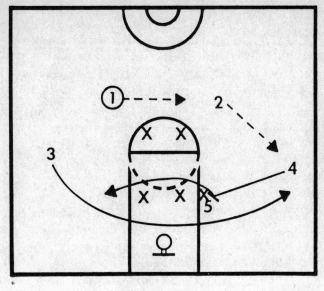

Diagram 5-8

executing a screen and roll with either wing man. This move may be run off the screen move by the guards as in diagram 5-6 or from just simple passing out front. If there is no play, the ball can be thrown out front to begin all over. Diagram 5-8 shows the use of the double screen in the 2-2-1. Wing 4 comes down to screen with 5 or 3. If there is no play for 3 or 5, any of the options may be used since the wings would have just traded positions. This offense offers baseline, wing, and guard screens. In addition, a weakside two-man game could be put in for 3 and 1 or 2 as an option in diagram 5-7. With a couple of good shooters and a big man that cannot do much more than rebound and shoot layups, it can help a limited team do some good against the conventional point defenses.

The Cutting Offense

This pattern is a bit involved, but can be very effective against the 2-3 zone and matching up defenses. Starting from a

2-3 set, 1 passes to 3 and cuts through, looking for a return pass. As 1 clears, 5 pops up out of the post and wing 4 looks for the best opening he can find in the middle. Guard 2 floats to a wider spot, hoping to free himself. If three can play with 1, 5, or 4, he does so, of course. He himself is isolated for a good one-on-one against a matchup, by the way. If 3 reverses the ball to 5, 5 will look for 4 or 2 quickly. But in diagram 5-10 we see another quick option coming with a cross under the goal motion. As 3 reverses the ball, he cuts into the lane, avoiding 4, and 1 comes back under. If 5 throws to either wing as in diagram 5-11, he will cut to the goal just as 1 did in diagram 5-9 and just as we prescribe for him in the free-lance game. At this point the offense can end and everyone resets to start over if nothing has happened. Or, as in diagram 5-11, a continuity pattern may result by having the new post man pop up to the point, the wing slide into the post, etc. In my opinion, continuity moves that go beyond two sides are not worth the effort they take to learn. It is so much easier to reset and start over, or better yet, go into free-lance.

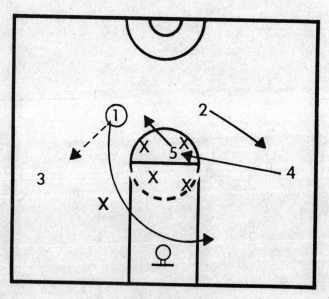

Diagram 5-9

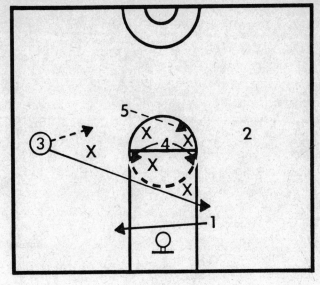

Diagram 5-10

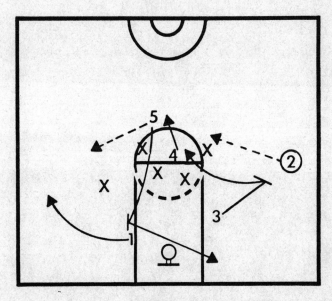

Diagram 5-11

The Triangle Move

This is a simple move that operates from nearly any starting formation. We will see it from the 1-3-1 and the 2-1-2. The purpose of the move is to create extra motion inside in an attempt to get the ball into that vital area. In diagram 5-12 the triangle moves counterclockwise as the ball goes to wing 2. Note that 2 drags the ball down a little in a pull move in order to set up a better passing angle inside. As he moves, 4, then 3, and finally 5 begin cutting in a triangle continuously, trying to get open. Each man watches the one in front of him in order to keep spaced and to give each man a chance not simply to run through the lane, but to make a legitimate effort to get open. Players 2 and 1 may pass the ball to each other two or three times while the three in the triangle attempt to free themselves. At any point that one of the players feel they are in a stalemate, the ball can be reversed to the other side. Player 1 may originate it with a dribble move or one of the triangle men can break out to the opposite wing as 4 does in diagram 5-13. When the ball is reversed, the original wing man gets into the triangle with the two remaining original triangle players. Diagram 5-14 illustrates the triangle from the 2-3 origination. The same principles apply exactly as in the 1-3-1 setup explained in the preceeding sentences. This is a simple move to learn and can be of some use in situations when the team wants to make an extra effort to get the ball inside.

The 1-2-2 Inside Move

This is an excellent move with two big men who cannot do much away from the goal or with only one big man to whom you want to get the ball inside during the game. In the latter case, the team needs to begin the offense opposite his low post position, however. Diagram 5-15 shows 1 passing to 2, who in turn feeds 4 in the corner. Player 2 uses the corner slide cut and screens 5, who must wait for the screen. If 4 can hit 2 or 5, he

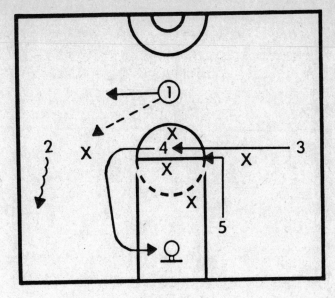

Diagram 5-12

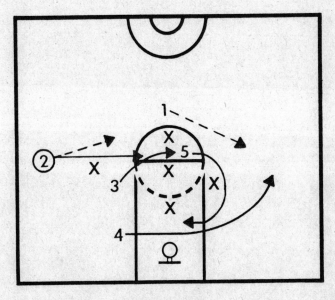

Diagram 5-13

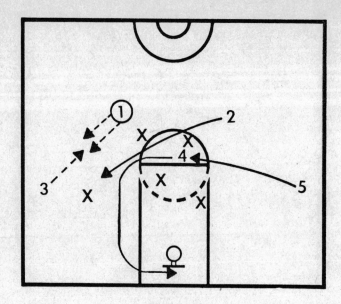

Diagram 5-14

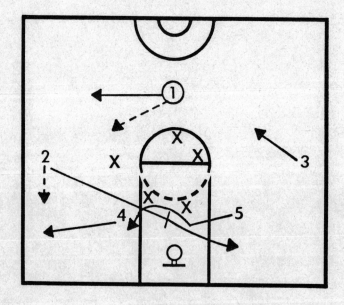

Diagram 5-15

does. If not, he reverses to 1 who has squared over. In Diagram 5-16 observe that 1 and 3 are in the normal guard positions and that as the ball is passed to 1 and then 3, 5 rolls up slightly and crosses in front of the goal, looking first to receive a pass from 1, and then from 3, and finally from 2. Thus, 5 has an opportunity to beat his man for the ball and get a pass from four different men. When well executed, 5 will find that he has a pretty good one-on-one shot at getting free from his man. Too much sagging by the defense will yield good medium range shots, and not enough will open the inside. In diagram 5-17 we see how the move can continue indefinitely if there are two capable inside men available. Post 5 pulls on out to the corner if he fails to receive the ball inside and the move is executed again, this time from the other side.

This play can be used very effectively in conjunction with two or three other plays from a 1-2-2 set. Such moves could include a dribble move, a pop the high post move when one of the low post men breaks high, and a baseline screen move.

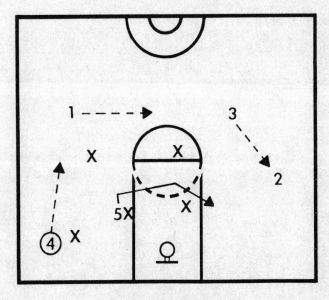

Diagram 5-16

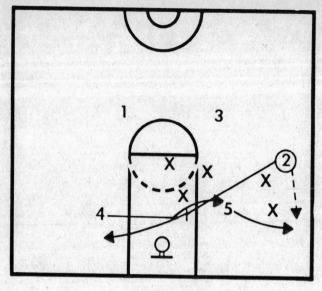

Diagram 5-17

These would make a four-part offense including the inside move just described here. The latter could be signalled by the key of the low post man pulling out to the corner. In fact, I have used the 1-2-2 this way in times past. The 1-4 also lends itself to taking two or three of the Basic Five moves, adding a special keyed play, and making it an entire offense. This may be done from the 1-3-1 as well, and it is made simple to accomplish when the players know the Basic Five moves in the first place. Actually, any coach could take the best zone breaker he has been using, from whatever formation, and add a few of the free-lance Basic Five options such as dribble-rotate, or the high-low exercises, or some screen move, and create a nice three- or four-part offense. Doing this with a couple of good moves would give a team quite an effective arsenal for the most part, I would think. It is the knowledge of the Basic Five and how to execute them that sets it all up and makes the rest easy.

6

Defeating the Laning Zones

The laning zones present a big threat to the offense because they defend aggressively and riskily, applying pressure to the passing game. In truth, when a team is skilled enough to go against the lane zones, the very affirmation that the zone is taking risks indicates that the offense can capitalize if they stay calm. But, like going against the presses which take even more risks, a physically or psychologically unprepared team will suffer against aggressive play.

The first problem is one of identification. Just as soon as someone realizes that the defense has begun to use laning tactics with its entire zone, or even partially, such as only when the ball is in the corner, the first player to realize it must let the rest of the team know. The reason for this is that in order to keep the ball moving, the offensive player in the area or areas being laned will have to adjust to penetrate the pass lanes. Remember in our earlier discussion of laning zone play that the offense must use a lot of punching, high-low post passing, and cutting to the holes between the lane defender and the goal, more or less backdoor style. Otherwise the offense will either be pushed too far out on the floor to run an effectively consistent attack or will be forced to lob passes slowly and dangerously over the lane defender's heads with little hope of good results. Certainly a team that has been attacking against the containing zones and confronts people in the lanes for the first time will be caught off-guard. So, the first point is to identify the problem. Next comes how to get the offensive job done against it.

Since laning tactics have become more popular in each of the last few years, one may expect to see even more of this defensive variation in the future, I would judge. In my mind, a change to laning from a containing or a matching defense creates more of a problem than when the opponent changes from 2-3 to 1-3-1 or from a standard zone to matching up. The reason is that most zones tend slowly to become alike as play progresses, anyway. Once the defense moves the ball past the original formation, most zones will adjust to about wherever the ball and players are. For instance, recall that all zones are alike in formation with the ball located in the corner. This is true of the lane zones too, with the exception that the player who is defending the wing man will be right upon him in an effort to try to keep the ball from being thrown successfully out of the corner to the reverse side. Still, good cutting and peripheral ballhandling will give the offense what it wants in the way of good shots against containing and matching zones, if the team has any patience at all.

This is not true against the lane zones. While patience for the good shot is still a virtue, the shot will come a little sooner against the lane defense when the execution is carried out, or else it may never come at all. Furthermore, the peripheral passing game will be broken up, pushed out, or slowed down with an effective lane zone. To compound the offensive problem, too much pattern-type, continuity cutting will not be effective against the men in the lanes.

To go against the lane attack, the offense must use quick-hitting passes to the interior of the defense at the moments in which they can penetrate behind the defenders in the lanes who have left their backside unprotected. If men are cutting rather haphazardly all over the offensive court, there will be no one in the open lanes when the ballhandler needs them. To attack the lanes, the ballhandler has to punch quickly and know that he will have alert men to flip to once he gets into the interior of the zone. The ballhandler must have an active high post man to give him an everpresent penetration possibility. And he has to keep a cool head with the ball at all times because the offense will not flow as well as against the containing zones; the ballhandler has to be aware to keep *turning the ball in,* to penetrate, or the game momentum can go to the defense in a hurry.

In this chapter I will re-emphasize the best Basic Five moves to go to when the defense gets into any or all of the lanes, and then give some special moves to utilize in the event the players are not performing effectively against the laner on their own. Regardless, the knowledge of the way a lane zone works and of the best free-lance moves to use against a laner will help any pattern or system to be more effective when facing this style.

Using the Basic Five

Some coaches will have their lane defense put one man directly on the ball and then try to push out into the two adjacent pass lanes while having the defender in the high post take the individual responsibility to keep the ball out of the high post area. Others will play two defenders on either side of the ball, offering an inviting gap to the ballhandler, while playing facing the ballhandler with their outside hands sticking out in the passing lanes. While the gap is there, the defense that plays in this manner is probably skilled at setting a good trap if the ballhandler makes a careless, too-deep penetration and is pressured before he knows what he wants to do with the ball. Regardless, it becomes a matter of execution and any defense that lanes will offer many gap-punching opportunities to the ballhandler. He should use these openings very often, just keeping in mind that he must be ready to move the ball before he gets too much defensive pressure. He cannot wait until he has attracted a crowd and then begin to figure out what to do with the ball.

Punching. In the first three diagrams we see some punching possibilities against laning zones in the 1-2-2, 1-3-1 and 2-1-2 formations respectively. In diagram 6-1 the offense has met the defense in 2-1-2 or else could have dribble-pulled from a 1-3-1 into the pictured positions. At any rate, 1 punches a gap in the front line and players 2, 3, and 4 read the situation to determine whether to move up or down. Recall in our discussion of punching earlier in Chapter Three that they do not want to move in very far, shutting off the pass angle. Post 5 makes his automatic move, according to our principles, stepping up to a very high post spot. In diagram 6-2 point 1 is covered, but angles inside, anyway, after a fake step, drawing the wing defender. Player 2 drops wisely, making it difficult for anyone to reach him. Post 4 steps up as before. Post 3 and wing 5 will read the situation for openings or rebounding. The wing player 2 finds a gap in diagram 6-3 and punches in. The posts both respond by pulling out a step or two each, while 1 gives an opportunity for an escape pass. Wing 3 reads for a wide pass or for rebounding.

Player 1 cannot move the ball in diagram 6-4 because his teammates are flatfooted and are caught by the alert defense. This is the situation the lane defense thrives upon. If 4 fails to break out, or if the wings stand still instead of trying to beat the defense, the ballhandler is stuck and will often panic. A cool head here can save the day and create a good opening if the ballhandler will exercise the one-on-one punch move. Wing 3 flares as the dribble move comes at him, while 4 pops up. Wing

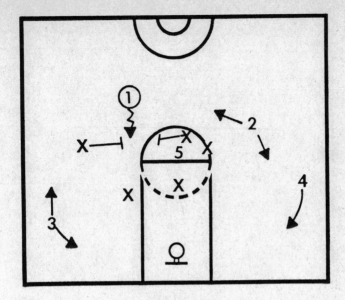

Diagram 6-1

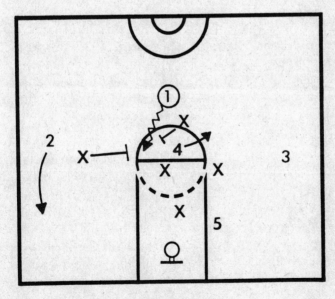

Diagram 6-2

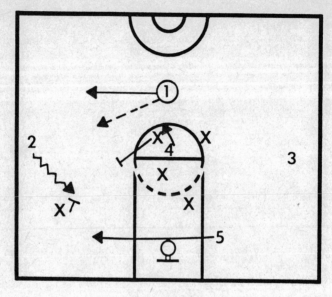

Diagram 6-3

2 reads as to whether to go up or down for an opening. This move will normally stir the other offensive players to move in the appropriate manner. It certainly will cause the defense to adjust. The opportunities to punch are innumerable. They should be used often with any offensive system, but should not be overused, especially by an unskilled ballhandler.

Dribble moves. Instead of using a penetrating punch in diagram 6-4, point 1 could have run a wide dribble-rotate move as in diagram 6-5 or a pop the post, illustrated in diagram 6-6. Observing the wide dribble to a new offensive slot, wings 3 and 2 make their necessary adjustments, with 3 roving the base if the ball is reversed. The posts also adjust accordingly to help create openings inside the zone. In diagram 6-6 the point takes only two quick bounces laterally, keying the post pullout with his dribble-pull exercise. The reader will easily identify the rest of the moves in this play, one which I feel is a defensive killer and a required weapon in the offensive arsenal. Diagram 6-7 gives the

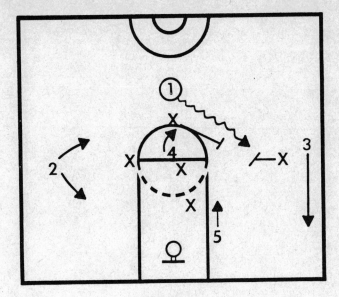

Diagram 6-4

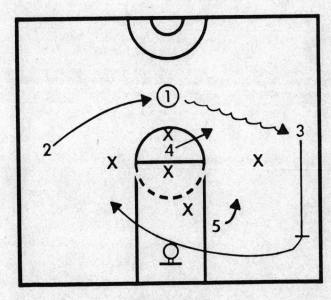

Diagram 6-5

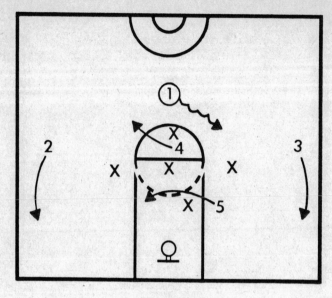

Diagram 6-6

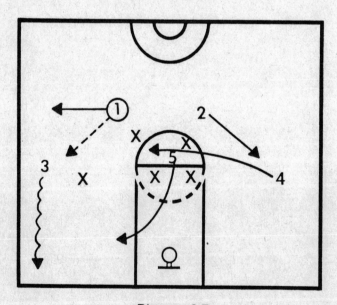

Diagram 6-7

wing dribble-rotate option. After going out wide to receive the pass, he turns the ball back toward the goal into better penetrating position. Point 1 gives him an outlet, and 5, 4, and 2 make clever adjustments as they read the defense. The dribble options give the ballhandler a better choice than throwing looping passes or trying to force a pass to someone who is not clearly open.

Cutting. It is impossible to show the innumerable possibilities to cut into the openings of the various defensive alignments, so we will view a few options from which generalizations may be made. Selecting a 1-2-2 set against a 2-1-2 laner in diagram 6-8, observe low post 5's flash cut to the inside of the wing-post pass lane. All the offensive players adjust to the pass, because the offense has a clear advantage with the ball in this position. It will be hard to cover 3 and 4 on the baseline, while 2 can free himself on the side opposite. In diagram 6-9 the same offensive alignment goes against the 1-3-1 defense. Wing 3 sees an opening in the point-wing lane. He will go as close to the ball as he must to get open. If he gets covered by the point defender, preventing his getting open, 1 has a good opening by cutting to the wing that 3 vacated. If the high post defender tries to deny 3, 5 can get open in the lane. Diagram 6-10 shows 3 getting the ball and the proper action on the backside in order to beat the defense. We see a simple backdoor exercise in diagram 6-11 as 3 fakes out against the forcing defensive tactics of his defender and cuts back to penetrate the pass lane. Once inside, he can pass to 4 or 5 who must read the defensive response. Once the ball is inside the pass lanes, it is obvious that the defense is at a disadvantage, having to pay for its risks.

High-low post action. The heart of any offense is the high-low post game, or at least the inside game, however it develops. This is doubly true against zones and, if possible, even more true in attacking the laning style of zones. It is the "without which nothing" of the laning game, offensively. Earlier, under the discussion of dribble moves, I mentioned the pop the post option, and this is also a part of the high-low post game, so there is no need to mention it further here. In addition, my presentation of

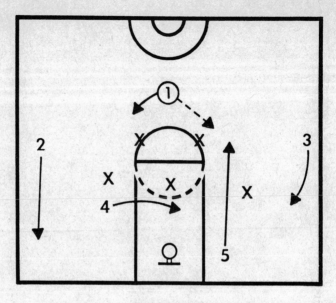

Diagram 6-8

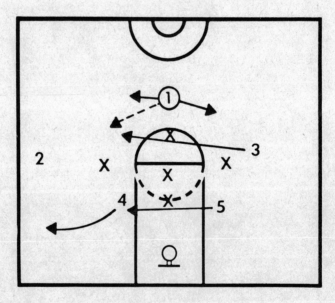

Diagram 6-9

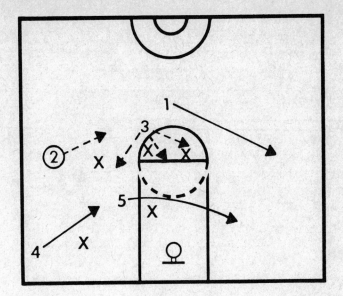

Diagram 6-10

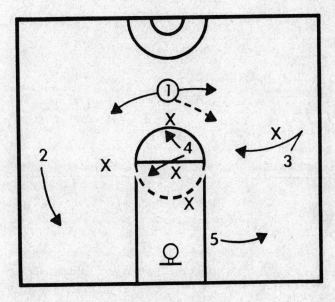

Diagram 6-11

the 1-4 offense against the lane zones later in this chapter will show a lot of post action. For now, we will look at only two pictures to describe the effects of some simple high post passes.

In diagram 6-12 point 1 gets the pass in to 4, who had to maneuver to get free. The other players react as in the pop the post move. In diagram 6-13 the wing feeds the ball to 4 who had to come up very high and wide, but he knows he must move a lot to get open. Post 4 turns and looks under and opposite to try to feed 5 or 3 quickly. It is important for the post men to know their responsibilities and options for movement as described in Chapter Three, under the discussion of the inside game. The post play can ruin lane zoning quicker and easier than any other exercise.

The forcing nature of the lane zones increases the need for spontaneous free-lance play. The team that can identify the zone and use quick-hitting cuts and punches will capitalize on the defensive gaps created by risks better than any pattern can. The special moves in the following paragraphs are good systems against the laners, but will be far more effective if players can read the openings and know about free-lance options instead of trying to play the patterns like robots.

The 1-4 Against Lane Zones

The 1-4 alignment has become very popular in recent years because it is so adaptable to various zone defenses and to the man-to-man, as well. Of course, it takes different moves to be effective against the separate defenses, but it is sometimes an advantage to be able to use different offenses out of the same formation. The defense does not notice offensive changes quite so readily when the same alignment is used, even if the pattern is changed.

Diagram 6-14 shows the high 1-4 positioning that is most effective against the lane zones. We use basically four moves in playing the lane defenses of any formation. This one offense is so effective against laning tactics that we have never had to go further in search of another pattern. It is tailor-made to suit

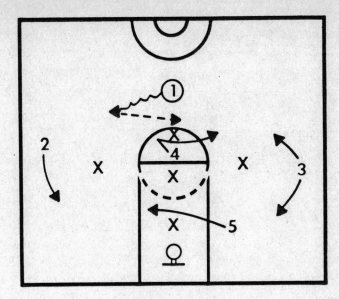

Diagram 6-12

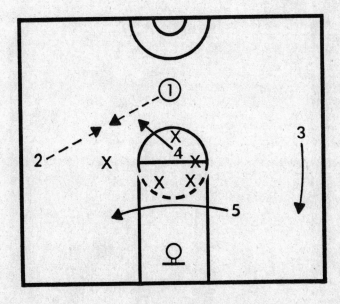

Diagram 6-13

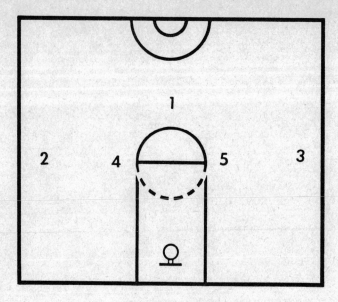

Diagram 6-14

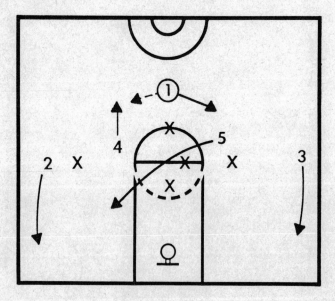

Diagram 6-15

laning zones. The first move in diagram 6-15 shows the post pass. If the ball goes to one post man, the other cuts to the goal and the wings drop to the base area. The point man moves to the opposite guard slot. This move puts tremendous pressure on the basket, because the defense is pushed out into the lanes. The success of this move depends on the willingness of the post men to keep moving up and down in the high and extremely high post areas in order to get free. They cannot get open on the foul line and work the move effectively, and they cannot stand still outside at the 22 foot mark if they are not open on the first attempt. Most teams that I have seen use this offense do not keep their posts either active enough or high enough.

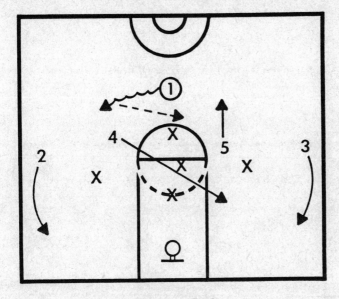

Diagram 6-16

The second move is the familiar pop the post move that we have added to every pattern when possible. There is no need to explain diagram 6-16 since it is so familiar by now, and the moves are the same as for diagram 6-15 after the point dribbles over a couple of bounces. Diagram 6-17 shows the third move, a

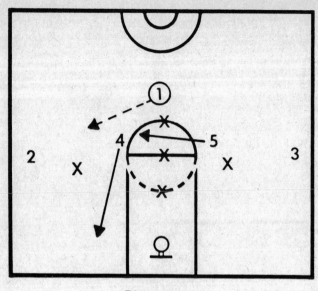

Diagram 6-17

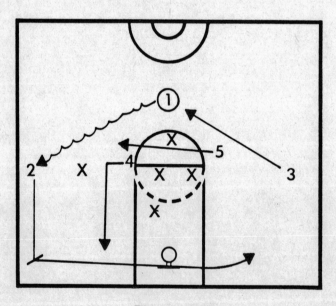

Diagram 6-18

pass to either wing. The posts roll to the ball side and the other three men hold position, although the ballhandler may punch or pull the ball. On the quick reversal of the ball, the posts execute a cross inside. If there has been no play by the time the ball is reversed, the original formation sets up again. The fourth option is to use a dribble move as in diagram 6-18. The point initiates the move in this diagram that again has a familar look to it, but the wings may begin the same move to the corner when they desire.

These four actions have always given us an effective attack against the laning zones. They give the opportunities to hit quickly on any punch moves available, to penetrate the high post readily, and to move the ball enough to give opportunities to crack inside the defensive gaps with cuts. It is a quick-hitting attack. For those interested in other possibilities with the 1-4 offense which can be used against the containing and matchup styles, I refer you to the next chapter, under the discussion of the high-low post against the matchups.

Naturally each coach will decide for himself what he believes his team needs in order to be well-prepared without being overcoached to the point that the players really know very little that they execute well. Whether a coach decides to use a new offense against the lane zones or not, I seriously recommend that he at least emphasize with all his ability the high post game, when he sees the opponent in the lanes, as an option to his regular offense. He should also warn his players to keep trying to turn the ball back in, so as to keep from getting pushed entirely out of their offense.

7

Coaching Against
the Matchup Zones

The matchup zones evolved in response to the offensive effectiveness of many of the overloading and pattern offenses used against the standard-moving zones. As noted earlier, the matchups are an attempt to utilize as much man-to-man as possible and still stay in a zone defense. Many coaches freeze when they see they are going to have to go against a matching zone. This is needless because the man who has no idea what to do against the matching style can still get a lot of mileage out of his regular man-to-man offense, provided it has the normal amount of screening and cutting. While there are better methods to attack, the man-to-man offenses are generally effective and the players can usually run them well because they are the most familiar single thing most teams know. If all else fails, I always recommend that a coach turn to his man-to-man offense, particularly early in a season. Of course, our purpose here is to show how the Basic Five and special plays can work against the matchups.

The Basic Five and the Matchups

Because of the desirability of matching up as opposed to having players standing around in an area where there are no offensive players, most defensive coaches are using some kind of matchup variation with their standard zones. That is, unless a defender wants to stand around guarding air, he will shift into a nearby area where he can cause the offense some trouble. Certainly some defenses will have as many as five or ten rules to cover all the cuts and screens that the coach expects to see thrown against him. A team that is well-coached and uses the matchup as its "bread and butter" defense can really cause any strict pattern team problems. Therefore, the free-lance option emphasis is very important in attacking the matchups. Just as soon as the offense realizes that it is being matched up either by intent or by accident, the team has to initiate a move or will have to play one-on-one without having too many really open shots.

Punching and dribble-moves. Punching is effective against any defender whenever a gap appears in the defense. There is no need to diagram punching and dribble-moves again here since they are the same as offered with the discussions of these exercises in the earlier chapters. I will simply emphasize that both moves are highly effective against the matchups. In fact, one of the keys that the ballhandler looks for in order to know when to use both the dribble-moves and the one-on-one punch move is noting when the defense has the offense matched up. The dribble moves cause the defense to have to rotate out of position in order to stay with the dribbler and the rotating cutters or else to go a step or two and release the ballhandler to the adjacent defender. If he does this, he must then react to pick up the new offensive man cutting into his area, who, in turn, must be released by the man who was guarding the area from which the cutter came. It is more difficult to match a quick dribble move than it is to match after most passes. As for the punching exercise, the very purpose of punching is to try to get two men to flex toward the ball, especially in the one-on-one punch, and if two men move toward the ball, certainly the defense is no longer matched up on all the offensive players.

Let us study one of my favorite patterns against the match-ups which utilizes the dribble-rotate and, of course, has options for punching as all plays must, in my opinion. The pattern starts in a 1-2-2 and the defense will match it up as in diagram 7-1. The ball may be passed around two or three passes before the dribble move is utilized. During that interim the posts can move in the post areas trying to get free and the outside men can look for punching and pulling opportunities as discussed in Chapter

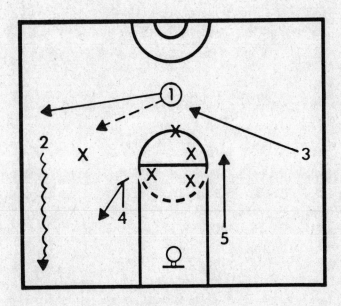

Diagram 7-1

Three. Any of the outside three men may initiate the dribble-rotate move that 2 starts in the diagram. The post on the ball side times his cut to the base by waiting for the dribbler to arrive in the corner. If 4 feels he cannot get open at all, he can go screen 5 and change cuts with him. Players 1 and 3 rotate behind the dribble and set up the reverse as in diagram 7-2. Note the post action in diagram 7-2. If there is no play, the offense is set to begin again.

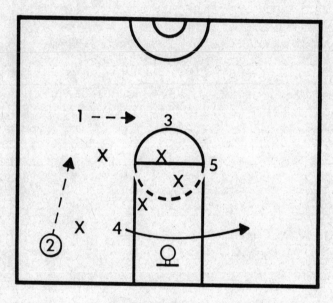

Diagram 7-2

Cutting. The easiest offense for the matchup to keep track of is the offense that stands around with little or no cutting. Let me digress a second here, however, just to mention that if the offensive team is superior to the defending team and if the offensive team has a good man or two on the inside, it might be able to win against the matchup by simply lining up in a 2-3 and working the ball in from the sides and using some reverse two-man games as variation. In other words, make the matchup play as much man-to-man as they want, if your players can go one-on-one successfully, anyway. If the offense fails, then the team can shift to a different attack. If it succeeds, the defense has to shift to a containing zone and leave openings somewhere other than in the post area. I think a team should win the simplest way it can, regardless of how it looks to have trick plays.

In cutting against the zone that is in matched positions, the offense must keep in mind the same rule that exists for the punching and dribble moves. That is, any time the defense seems to have the offense in stymie position, when the passing is difficult because everyone is covered, or when there seems to be stagnation in the offensive motion, one of the proper moves is either the give and go pass and cut or a simple free-lance cut to an open area. These moves all create offensive motion and cause defensive adjustment. In either case openings are more likely to happen for the offense.

For emphasis I would like to call attention to two moves here that predicate on cutting. The first of the patterns is the "point cut and wing cross" shown in diagrams 7-3 through 7-5.

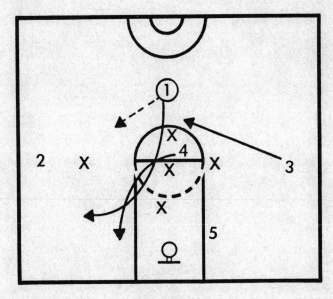

Diagram 7-3

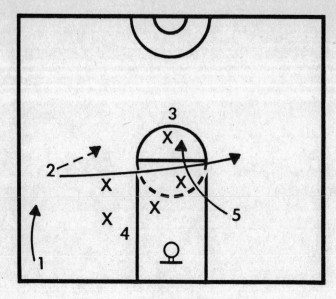

Diagram 7-4

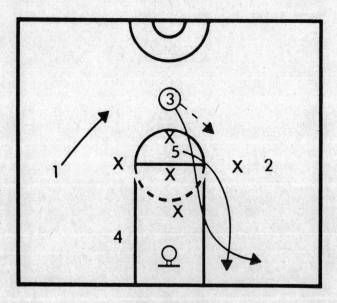

Diagram 7-5

In the first of the diagrams the point passes to a wing and cuts to the corner, looking out for a return pass. On this move 2 will not cut if he throws to 1 in the corner, only when he reverses the ball to the top. If he passes to 1, he holds position. On the reversal, as shown in diagram 7-4, 2 makes a quick cut to the open wing area opposite and 5 cuts right off of his tail, while 1 slides up to the other wing. If the ball goes into the post, the pattern becomes a regular high-low post game. If the ball goes to either wing, as it is shown in diagram 7-5, the play continues as in the first picture, 7-3. These cuts cause a lot of adjustment by the defense if they are run quickly. The move has both inside and outside options.

Diagrams 7-6 and 7-7 illustrate a second simple offense that utilizes cutting effectively against the matchups. The move may be called the "posts cross and corner slide." From a 1-3-1 set, wing 2 passes to post 4, who has pulled to the corner. He could pass to 5 who cuts to the high post as 4 leaves. After passing, 2

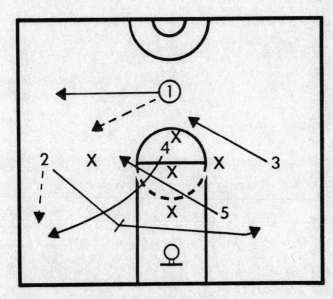

Diagram 7-6

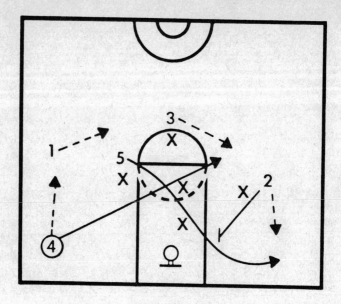

Diagram 7-7

uses the corner-slide move and posts up momentarily before clearing on to the opposite side. If the ball reverses, as in 7-7, the posts complete their cross move. As 2 gets the ball on the reverse side, he may feed either post man. If there is no play, the whole process may be started over again with 2 passing to the new corner to 4 and cutting again.

Another cutting pattern would be "The Cutting Offense," in Chapter Five. There, diagrams 5-9 through 5-11 illustrate a very effective offense against matchups.

Screening. Because of the man-to-man aspects of matching up, it is only natural that a man-to-man exercise such as screening would prove to be worthwhile. Before examining further suggestions here, I refer the reader back to two offensive patterns that use screening that are effective against the matchups: the "Baseline Pinch" in diagrams 5-1 and 5-2 of Chapter Five, and the "2-2-1 Screener" in diagrams 5-6 through 5-8 in the same chapter.

The 1-2-2 Jam

In this offense the principles of staying wide on the weak-side and of keeping the inside open are thrown out the window. This may be a reason not to use it. On the other hand, depending on your outlook, it may be just the reason to throw it in. At any rate, the offense squeezes the defense right up to the foul lane area.

In diagram 7-8 we see the point pinch and post screen opposite option as 1 uses 2's screen and 4 bumps for 5. Players 2 and 3 rotate off of a second screen as shown. If there is no play, the offense is ready to begin again with players having traded starting spots. Diagram 7-9 shows the wing cross move. Wing 2 squeezes in and cuts out for a pass. When he gets it, 3 cuts under 4's screen. If 2 passes the ball to 3 or 4, he crosses to the other side. Post 5 times his cut up to see if he has an opening depending on the defense. He may be open just after 3's cut. If not, he

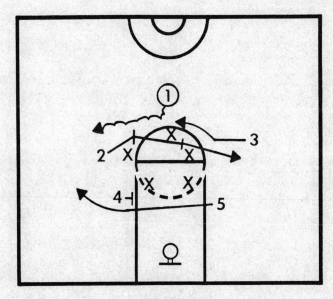

Diagram 7-8

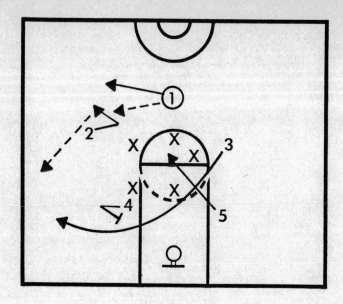

Diagram 7-9

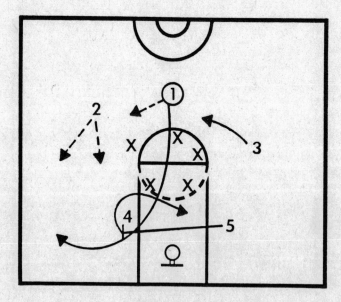

Diagram 7-10

can try to cut up when 1 gets the ball on the reverse, after 2's cut. If there is no play, the men are in the 1-2-2 positions and ready to go again. The last diagram of the set (Diagram 7-10) shows the post double screen and guards cross play. On signal, the posts line up on the same side of the lane. The point quickly passes to the wing on that side and cuts off of the double screen. As 1 clears the screen, the low man, 5, cuts to the goal as well. When wing 2 feeds, he rotates to the other side quickly and the offense is ready to go again. The jamming action offers many medium range options and has good rebounding. Also, if the screens are not negotiated defensively, there will be quick openers to the post men setting the screens.

The High-Low Game

Again, I would ask the reader to refer back to the discussion of the high-low post game in Chapter Three for proper appreciation of the value of the inside game. In addition, the aforementioned moves such as popping the post, "The Cutting Offense" of Chapter Five, and the 1-4 Offense, as described in Chapter Six, are all good examples of post action that will work effectively against the matching zones. The 1-4 has proven especially effective as an offense. In addition to the plays that work against the lane zones shown in the preceeding chapter, which also work against matchups, I want to present further possible options using the 1-4 set.

Screening the point is shown in diagram 7-11. Posts 4 and 5 offer a choice of screens for the point. He selects 4 and drives off, looking for a shot, or for 2 flaring, or for 4 on the roll. Post 5 and wing 3 move as shown to give a reverse outlet and more pressure on the goal. The point cut option is illustrated in diagrams 7-12 and 7-13. Point man 1 can cut to either corner and 3 rotates behind him while the posts slide to get open. In diagram 7-13 the point has received the ball in the ballside corner and we see the reverse action as 1 throws to 2 and goes baseline as the posts cross. If there is no play, the offense can begin again with 3 on the point. Twice through this offense will cause the defense a world of problems.

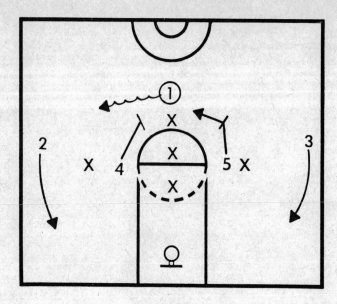

Diagram 7-11

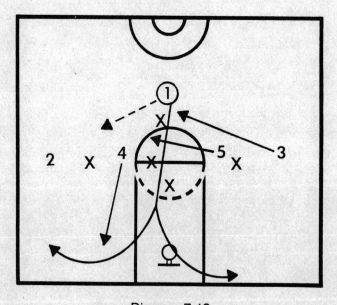

Diagram 7-12

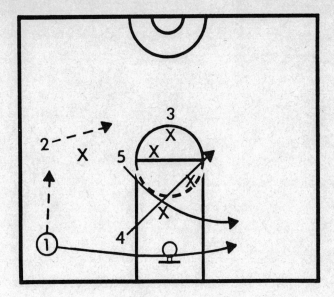

Diagram 7-13

The last extra move that I will deal with here is the post pull to the corner exercise. In diagram 7-14 post 4 pulls to the corner and gets the ball from 2, who then cuts to the goal looking for the ball on the corner slide. For variation, 5 can come wide for the release instead of 1, if desired. On the reverse, as shown in diagram 7-15, 1 may be open or he can try to feed 2 or 3 on the screen move down low. There are many more options available, but one can see the possibilities and can also observe how all the above employ the Basic Five moves.

The 1-2-2 Wide Offense

The 1-2-2 formation offers many options, but we will confine ourselves to some simple ones that can be taught easily and which go well with our system. First of all, the posts may screen for each other at any time and they may slide up and screen and roll with the wing man on their respective sides at will. Fur-

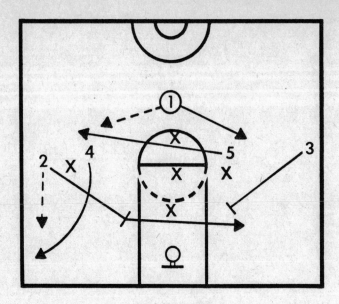

Diagram 7-14

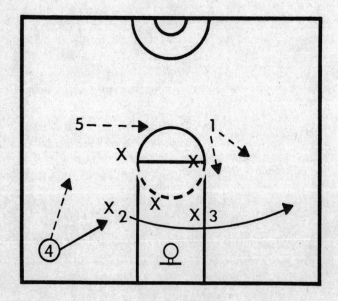

Diagram 7-15

thermore, either may cut high into the post area to initiate a high-low post game when he sees a gap to cut into or that the point is stuck with the ball. Another move that the posts may be allowed to employ would be the pull out to the corner to allow the wing to run a corner slide play. The wings look for punching and post cutting opportunities and can use dribble moves when the occasion arises. In addition, either may play a two-man screen game as shown in diagram 7-16 by moving to screen the

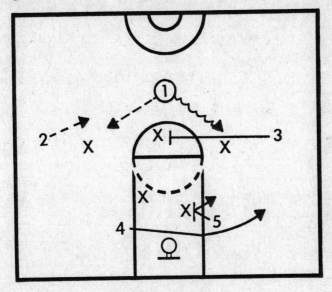

Diagram 7-16

point man when the ball is on the opposite side. The posts can cross for extra possibilities. Of course, the point has charge of the offense and can punch, cut, or use dribble moves when he feels the need. The 1-2-2 can become a nearly complete adjustable all-round offense like the 1-4 or 1-3-1, if the players are taught how to exercise the proper options when the defense contains, or gets matched up, or begins to jump out into the lanes.

The Wild Card

Eric Geldart of Western New England College used this offense well in his coaching in Puerto Rico in the summer league there. With a good player at the 3 spot as shown in diagram 7-17, it can be a good pattern against the matchups. Player 3 can cut to either wing, or can get the ball in the high post for that matter, if he is open. The guard on the side he cuts to, 2 in the diagram, passes and cuts through as 1 slides over and 4 moves up to the side high post. Player 3 can make a move or feed 5. If 5 is not open, he clears to the opposite post area. Incidently, I emphasize 4's move because this man is open often on the reverse pass as shown in diagram 7-18. Upon throwing the reverse pass, 3 cuts hard across the lane off of 5's screen. If there is no play for 2, 3, or 5, it is just as well to start over. Of course, more continuity could be added with a corner-slide cut by 2, etc. But it is a good move as it stands and there is nothing wrong with starting over, unless you are behind on the 30-second clock. The answer for that is to allow straight free-lance after the play has been attempted once through.

Screen the Top and Bottom

Starting from a 1-3-1 as in diagram 7-19, the point passes to 3, who in turn passes to 5 in the corner, and uses the corner-slide move. The high post does not roll down as he usually does unless he has such a clear opening he cannot pass it by. The ball reverses out of the corner and 1 drives to the weak side off of 4's screen as in diagram 7-20. At this time wing 2 puts a screen on 3 and 1 has the option to shoot, pass to 4 on the roll or to feed either 2 or 3. If there is no play, the men slide right back into 1-3-1 and begin again.

Before closing out the section on stunting defenses, I would like to add that against the zone and chaser/chasers defenses, I have used the man-to-man offense with such success that I be-

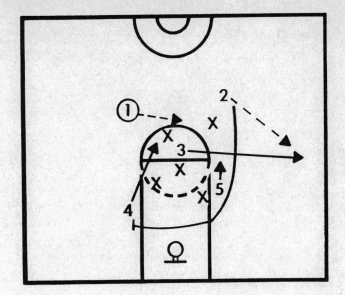

Diagram 7-17

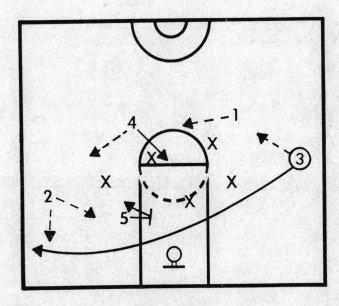

Diagram 7-18

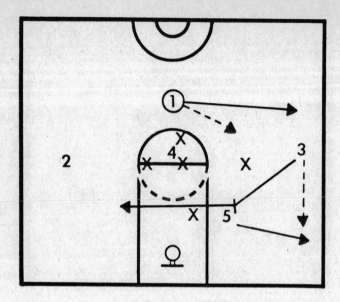

Diagram 7-19

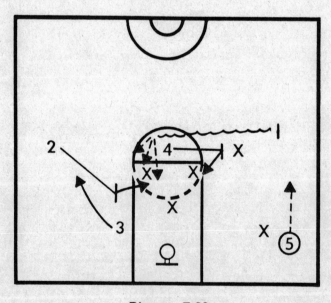

Diagram 7-20

lieve that most good cutting and screening man-to-man offenses offer the best panacea for those desperation defenses.

In concluding the discussions about attacking containing, laning, and matching zone defenses, I hope that it is clear that I believe the principles of zone offense in Chapters One and Two and the Basic Five moves in Chapter Three will bring success to a team's zone attack. While I believe players should have the first chance to beat zones on the strength of their knowing which of the Basic Five moves to use as the defense adjusts, the coach should have a few special moves to select from to help get good shots when the defense is getting the better of the player's execution or judgment. Although I do not believe there is any one offense that will beat all the zone variations, I do think that a coach can select one formation from which to use the Basic Five moves and to utilize a few moves as specific patterns from that same alignment in order to get the desired effects against the opponent whether he is laning, containing or matching up. On the other hand, I find it quite acceptable to use varying beginning formations, because executing the Basic Five is virtually the same regardless of the initial alignment.

In the next chapter I will deal with presses at half- and full-court. In doing so, we will consider how to get the quick fast break and to get the ball into the scoring area in order to use the half-court principles. Going against the presses requires a good bit of free-lance and the ability to play a broken offensive game. A strict pattern team that cannot adjust some on its own will suffer greatly at the hands of good pressing defenders. This is another reason why I believe in the Basic Five. It helps players to be able to capitalize on openings in the risk-taking presses.

8

Coaching Zone Offenses Against the Half- and Full- Court Zone Presses

The presses can devastate an ill-prepared opponent, but a team that is ready psychologically and fundamentally to go against presses can capitalize on the risk-taking of the defense. Presses are usually employed because the defending team wants to speed up the tempo of the game in order to break up the opponent's patterns or to catch up on the scoreboard. There are other reasons why a team might choose to press, but basically, the pressing team hopes to take some calculated risks to create errors and/or panic in the offensive attack. The first step in preparing a team psychologically is to explain that when the opponent places two men in trapping positions on the ball, there has to be an easy opening if the offense stays calm. Physically, the good teams will practice ballhandling sufficiently in order to be able to penetrate all the good defenses. If a team is in good physical condition, it only takes one more ingredient to be successful against pressing. That need is offensive organization. Confidence, good ballhandling, and organization will negate the presses and turn them into an offensive advantage.

Seven Steps to Beat the Press

Just as in any offensive or defensive attack, there have to be some basic principles behind what is done. Following are seven points that will help whatever formation or pattern that is utilized to work against the presses. Without the concepts or methodology, the patterns alone will not get the ball up the floor. It is the knowledge of these principles that will afford the necessary confidence to the offense. Application of these ideas will add to the ballhandling effectiveness, as well. That leaves it up to the coach to be sure his team does not lose to the presses because of being out of condition.

1. *Spread the offense.* The closer the offensive players bunch together in an effort to bring the ball into play, the easier it is for the defense to guard them. The smaller the area to defend, the better for the defense. A spread offense forces the defense to worry about the larger area. It is good policy to try to bring the ball into play with as few players as possible. I like to keep two men in positions where they can put fast pressure on our basket once we get the ball in play, so that the defense has to worry about defending our goal. If all of the offense crowds around the ball, the defense can add extra pressure, because it need not worry about covering the full defensive area. We hope to attack the press with three men and use two for a quick goal attack. However, if either the fourth or fifth man has to come up to get the ballhandler out of trouble, he will. When an opponent

is pressing, it is usually best to let the ball lay out of bounds before picking it up, to let the offensive players get organized and to have time to spread themselves out from each other. In my many years of coaching press defenses, I had a much easier time defending the teams who rushed the ball in bounds as quickly as possible before the men had a chance to spread and organize.

2. *Keep the ball in the air.* Players should always look to pass just as soon as they receive the ball, unless they are already under the goal for a layup. Most players tend to catch the ball, start dribbling and then look to see what to do with the ball next. The player catching the ball must look immediately up the court to try to avoid charging and to pass to an open man ahead. Dribbling is the last resort. Any press coach knows that the thing he wants to see the offense try against the press is a lot of dribbling. The dribbler allows the defense to focus in on the ball and to forget about the adjustments that quick passing causes. The chronic dribbler is the defense's best friend. If he kills the dribble under pressure, he might just as well change uniforms. Look to pass first, dribble as a last effort only.

3. *Use short, quick passes.* The long pass has almost no place in offensive basketball. Only if there is a man clearly open down long with no defender within 20 feet should a player try to throw long. Even then, I don't like long passes. I would gladly trade all the baskets my teams scored on long passes in 15 years for all the balls we threw away trying to get those goals. Avoid the long passes like a plague. Discourage throwing the ball to anyone who is running away from the ballhandler and emphasize the idea of meeting every pass with at least a half-step. Teams that look to pass first and who then execute short, quick passes to receivers who constantly meet the pass are more than half-way home against the presses. Meeting short, firm passes will cover a multitude of errors.

4. *Keep a safety man against the zone presses.* The offense should employ a triangle with the three men who are bringing the ball into play whenever possible. The man with the ball forms one point and a man a step or two behind ball level and 10

to 20 feet spaced from the ball forms the second. The third point will be filled by the other man helping the attack. If the ball is on a side, this man will be in the middle lane of the court. If the ball is already in the middle, this man will be in either outside lane and ahead of the ball level spaced 15 or 20 feet from the ball. It is important to have the safety man back so that when a trap closes in on the ball, the ballhandler does not have to throw through the trap necessarily. He may throw an easy escape pass backward. The release man may then reverse the ball up the other side of the floor normally, because the entire defense will have adjusted toward the ball in the trap. However, we prefer attacking, advancing passes.

5. *Attack under control.* It is important psychologically that the offense believes that it is going to attack the defense and make it pay the price for pressing and attempting to put two men on the ball and still cover the entire floor, or at least 50 feet of it. Yet, as important as it is to be aggressive and to try to penetrate for the easy goals, the byword must be "control." Control means going quickly, but being able to come to a stop to avoid charging. It means advancing the ball without careless errors and travels, and to be able to get the good shot without rushing into taking whatever kind becomes available. Control the mind and the body against the presses.

The attack should be made through the middle as much as possible. The presses are more effective on the sides because of the help the out of bounds lines afford. If the ball is not in the middle, and there is no offensive man in the middle trying to get open for a pass, the first man who notices this, except the safety man behind the ball, should cut immediately to that area. It is vitally important to attack from the middle because that is exactly where the defense does not want the ball to be. Say what you will, any team that is able to get the ball to the middle against any kind of defense will cause it a lot of trouble.

A last point on attacking is to keep moving toward the goal as the ball advances up the floor so that the entire offense is in attacking positions. The only time to go back toward the ball is if there is no offensive player in the middle in order to fill that hole or to go back to help a ballhandler who is in trouble. The key sentence to remember would be: "Advance as the ball advances; go back to it *only* if there is trouble."

Teams who attack in the middle, who stay spread and advance as the ball moves down court, will get a lot of quick attacks on the goal such as three-on-two or two-on-one.

6. *Get organized in the scoring area.* While it is necessary to look for the quick penetration, the offense must avoid taking many quick shots before the rest of the offense is prepared for rebounding. Only in certain conditions should a team try to win against the press without slowing down the offense in the scoring area. The prime example is when a team has so much offensive momentum that seemingly every shot is finding the range. There may be a few other instances but, basically, the run and gun against the press is poor policy if it allows too much outside shooting before getting set. This is a part of remaining cool under pressure. The defense normally wants the offense to step up the pace, so do not play into their hands.

7. *Read the defensive adjustments at half-court.* There are two things the defense can do as it falls back into the scoring area. It may drop into a conventional defense of either man-to-man or zone, or it may continue to press and trap even in the scoring area. That is, the defense may "settle" or it may continue pressing. The players, particularly the guards, must observe quickly how the defense is responding. If the defense settles, the offense can go right into the appropriate offense for the settled defense. If, on the other hand, the defense continues to chase the ball, the offense will probably have to use a more broken, or free-lance, game, or else a quick-hitting offense the coach has devised for such situations. Straight continuity patterns will be of little use normally. This is where organization at the half-court level becomes so crucial.

Entering Into the Offense Against Half-Court Presses

The first step to organization is to get the ball into the scoring area safely and then to look for the easy, quick basket.

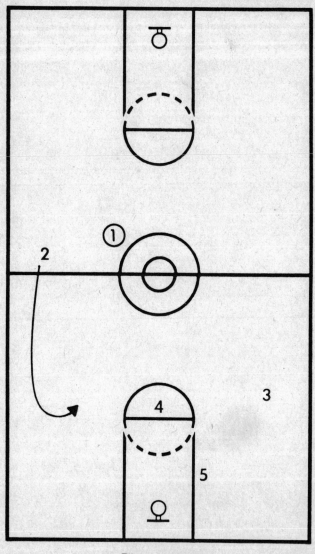

Diagram 8-1

(We will treat setting up patterns at half-court later in the chapter.) The first order of business is to get the ball inside, away from the half-line. In diagram 8-1 the offense enters with a 1-3-1 formation. Point 1 hesitates before crossing the half-line in order to let his running-mate, 2, get ahead to play the wing in the 1-3-1. Since the half-line is so close, there is no safety man in this case. (It is just like when the ball is out of bounds against the full-court press.) Point 1 now has a choice of three men to throw the ball to in the front court. One word of caution: players 2, 3, and 4 must begin near to the foul line extended level. If they start too near the half-line they are likely to receive the pass from 1 in a position so close to the line that the defense can put a trap on easily. In diagram 8-2 the ideal penetrating pass options are shown. The idea is to try to get the ball to the middle and then to attack under. This attack is best against a two-front press.

Diagram 8-3 shows another method of entering the scoring area, quite effective against point alignment presses. Guard 1 passes to either 5 breaking up or to wing 3. In either event, wing 4 and guard 2 break down to goal pressuring positions and 3 or 5 would look to penetrate quickly. If 1 cannot pass into 5 or 3 as in diagram 8-4, he throws reverse to 2 who stays back three or four steps in this move. Guard 2 then passes to either 5 or 4 and the operation is the same as in the preceding diagram.

The 1-4 can be effective as a method of entry against either the one or two-front defenses. It allows more entry options, but is slower to pressure the goal. In diagram 8-5 point 1 passes to the wing 2 and the posts roll down for penetration possibilities. Diagram 8-6 illustrates the pass to post 4 and the penetrating cuts by 2, 5, and 3.

Any of these options are effective, for they give good passing lanes, organization, and allow for quick capitalizing if the defense takes too much risk.

Entering into the Offense Against Full-Court Presses

As mentioned earlier, I prefer that the team wait and set up to get the ball down-court against the full press. In fact, I use a

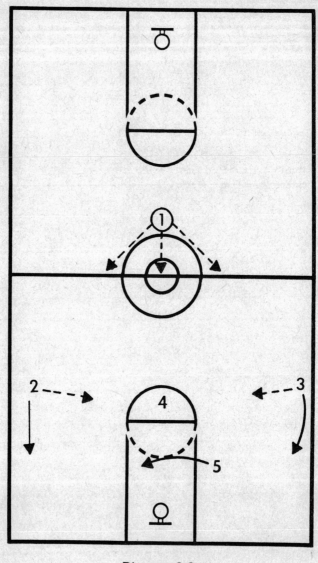

Diagram 8-2

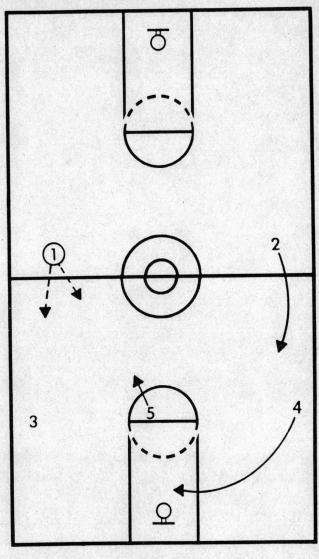

Diagram 8-3

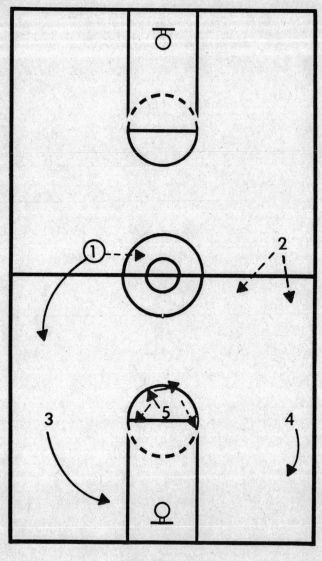

Diagram 8-4

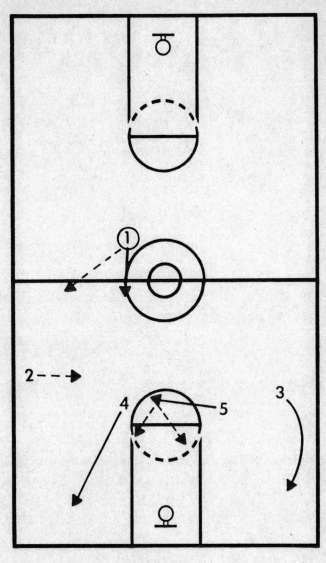

Diagram 8-5

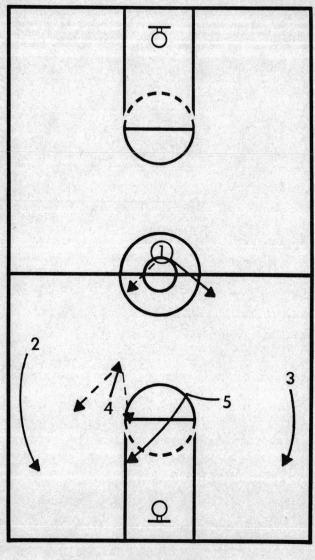

Diagram 8-6

designated man to throw the ball in bounds each time and have two other designees to be the two men to come to our front court, pressuring our own basket. I lost two important games despite all this when men who were supposed to go down court threw the ball inbounds instead, and in each case before anyone had a chance to organize, they threw it right to the opponent. Even the best laid plans. . . .

I prefer to attack every full-court press with the 2-1-2 pattern shown in diagrams 8-7 through 8-9. In the first of the diagrams we see the alignment. Players 2 and 3 line up on the foul line and may break out on their own. They can screen, cross, or go straight. If they are being pressured for the first pass, they must go right against their defenders and break back to the ball. They try to get open without going too close to the end-line, but will go right up next to the man out of bounds, if necessary. Remember that 1 wants to be sure to avoid being right under the basket when he takes the ball out of bounds. Players 4 and 5 go to the 2/3 court level and will break back to the ball only if the ballhandler gets into trouble. Diagram 8-8 illustrates the rule that if 2 gets the inbounds pass, 3 breaks to the middle. Of course the opposite is true if 3 gets the pass. Player 1 is the safety man. Should 2 have to pass back to 1, he would then have to move backward to a position two or three steps behind 1 so as to keep a safety. If 1 should get the pass from 2, his move would be to pass to 3 in the middle or to 5 who would have to come back a little to meet the ball. This quick reversal is often quite effective. In diagram 8-9, 2 needed help from 4. Note the moves by 5 and 3 to keep the quick attack possibilities in both 8-8 and 8-9.

There are any number of ways a coach may decide to set up against the presses. Keeping in mind that one way is about as good as another if the seven steps are employed, let us take a look at a few more attempts at organization by way of formation. In diagram 8-10 the lineup is 1-2-1-1. After 1 throws into 2 on the wing or to 3 in the middle, he moves to the opposite wing and stays behind ball level. The offense moves the ball to the middle as quickly as possible and attacks from three lanes.

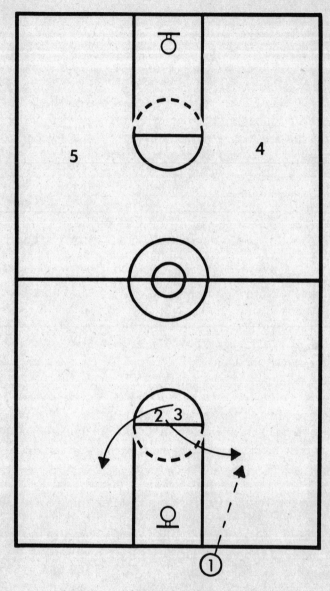

Diagram 8-7

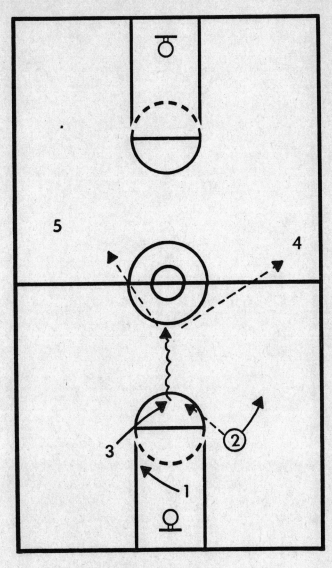

Diagram 8-8

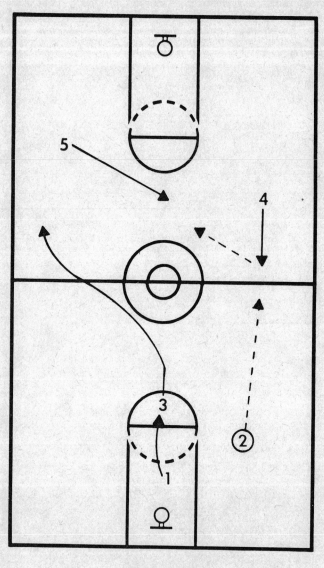

Diagram 8-9

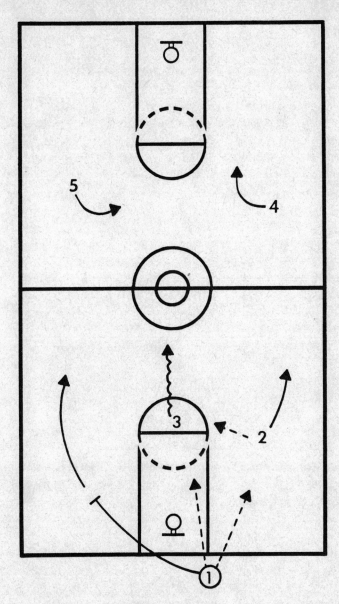

Diagram 8-10

Players 4 and 5 are alert for openings. In diagram 8-11, players 2 and 3 had to move to get open, so 1 has to take the other open lane as he steps in. Diagram 8-12 shows a 1-2-2 alignment with the front men using an optional cross move while 4 breaks up into the middle. As the ball is inbounded, they try to get the ball to the middle and attack up the three lanes. Player 1 remains as the safety man. Staying with the same formation in diagram 8-13, we see a good move called "cut behind the trap," or "the hook move." If the ball is thrown into 3, 2 will cut to a spot about 15 feet behind the ball. The point is the safety man and moves to the side 2 left, while 4 pressures the middle. Ballhandler 3 now has a middle option, a safety valve and a new option. That is, he can drop the pass right behind the trap oftentimes and beat the two trappers very quickly. If 2 is careful to cut to a spot close enough to the trap to make it difficult for the defender playing the downcourt pass to get to him, it is a safe move. After all, that same man has to watch player 5. Diagram 8-14 shows the same move to the opposite side of the floor. This move is excellent when employed against half-court pressure, too. The free guard simply hooks in front of the ballhandler before the ball crosses the half-line.

Diagram 8-15 shows the diamond rotate move. The players inbounds line up in a diamond, 1-2-1. If 1 takes the ball out on their left side of the goal, they all rotate to the left first one slot as shown, and then would continue rotating if no one is open on the first slide. Notice that the man in the spot 3 is in can go back long or just to the middle (which I prefer). Player 1 cuts into the open wing and becomes a safety. As the ball progresses up the floor the players remember to try to keep attacking into the middle. The following diagram shows the rotation to the right side of the floor. (Diagram 8-16, p. 180).

Staying Organized in the Scoring Area

Whether going against a half- or full-court press, the offense faces the same problem of re-organizing at the scoring-area level. If the press-breaking organization produces a good shot, the problem is eliminated, but this is not going to happen

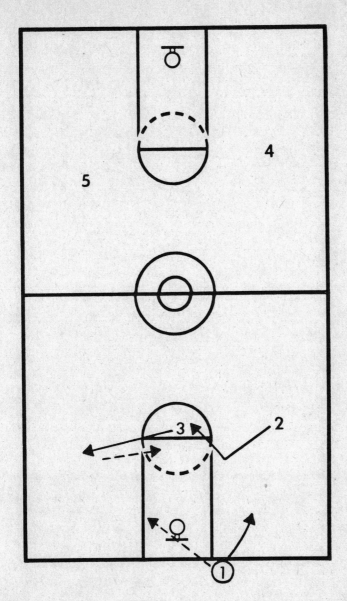

Diagram 8-11

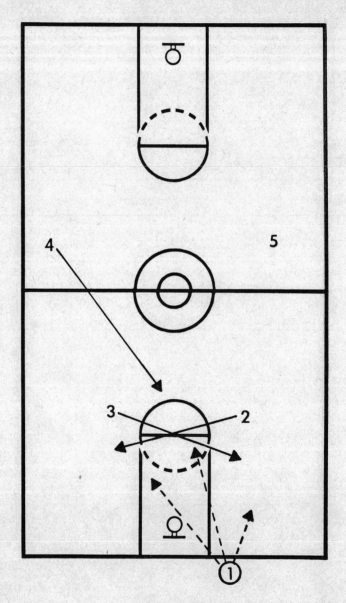

Diagram 8-12

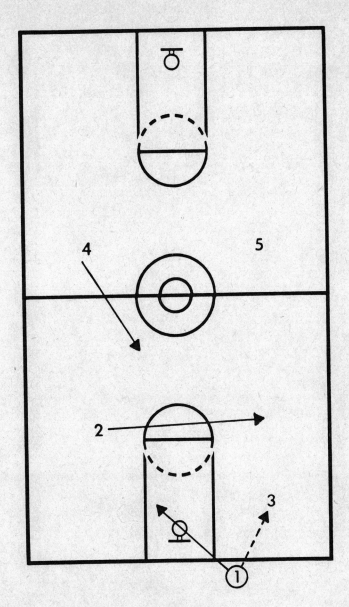

Diagram 8-13

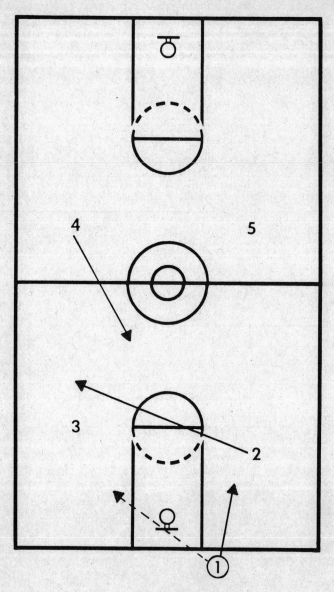

Diagram 8-14

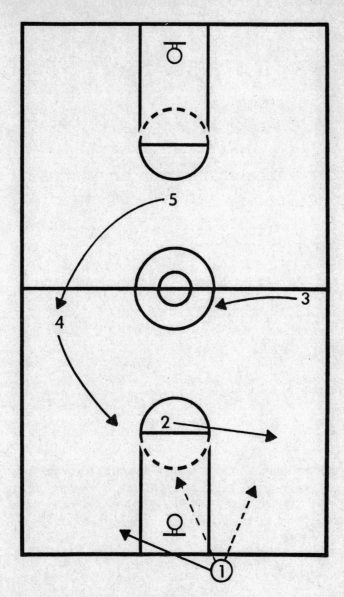

Diagram 8-15

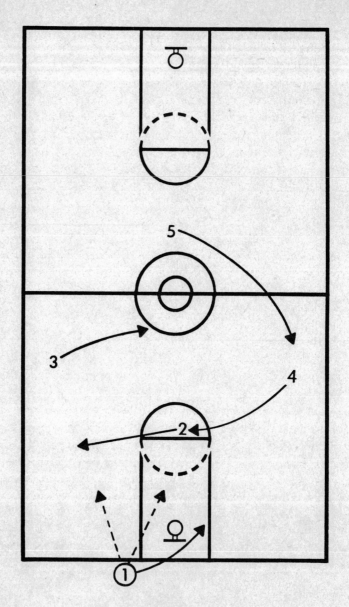

Diagram 8-16

often enough over the season. The press-breaker has done its job when it gets the ball into the scoring area safely. Any quick points it produces are a bonus. With the exception of those bonus points, it is not to the offense's advantage to continue in a rush. Panic must be avoided.

The key to organization at the scoring area level is not so much the kind of offense used, though that is important, but having the players recognize whether the defense settles to playing a regular defense, or if it continues to trap. If the former is the case, it is simply a matter of moving the ball to approximately the foul-line extended level, and then bringing it back out front for the guard to start the offensive pattern. Taking the ball to the foul-line will break the pressure because the defense must fall back. As long as the ball remains out front without this penetration, many defenses will stay right after it. Take it down and then set it up! What offense to use once the ball is brought out front again depends on whether the defense is in man-to-man or zone. It is as though the opponent had never pressed in the first place.

The team that continues to press in the scoring area, or indeed, the team who starts a trapping defense in the scoring area in the first place, presents a different problem. Against the scoring area trapping defenses, the continuity patterns are nearly useless. I have seen teams lose late-game leads by trying to run some stall pattern with continuity against zone trapping that was originally designed for man-to-man defenses. The offense must be able to play a more broken style of game, a quick-hitting high post action game that uses a lot of free-lance. The best moves for this are the 1-3-1 and the 1-4 as shown in the discussion of the lane zone offense in Chapter Six. The same may be accomplished with a spread 2-1-2. The only exceptions are that the guard dribble moves will not be effective against the traps and that the offense can afford to spread out more against the trapping defense to make them have to cover as much of the floor as possible. The whole offensive idea must be to take the ball to the middle and then under, or to the side, then the middle, and under. As in diagram 8-17, post man 4 must keep

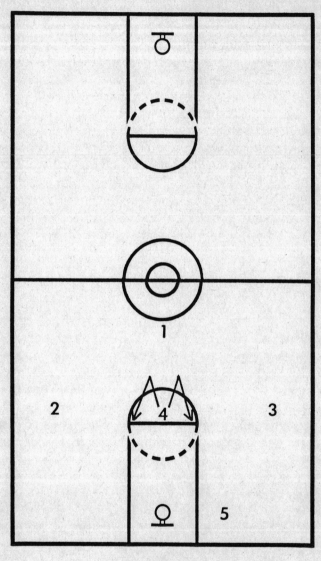

Diagram 8-17

active while the outside men look for him. A big key to remember is that if the ball is thrown inside and there is no shot, the ball should be taken out front quite high. Many teams will start attacking the traps spread out and then, once the ball gets inside, they move in and stay in. This allows the trappers to be able to continue their pressing, and just when they might be getting tired, they find that they have less ground to cover. If the ball comes back out front after the penetration, bring it high and make the defense come after it to open up again. Then go back in behind it until the team gets what it wants.

A thorough knowledge of and confidence in the Basic Five moves will give the offensive team the kind of knowledge it takes to bring success against all the various zones. If a coach will take the time to mimeograph the concepts on two or three pages and will give moderate practice time to them, the dividends will be very satisfactory.

9

Specific Drills
for Zone Offense

1. Passing drills. Pass around the horn and into the post. Six players stand in positions as shown in 9-1. Only player 6 can move around. Practice the following items in the drill: overhead passing, every third or fourth pass goes to the high post, outside players set the inside foot toward the goal, look at the goal when you get the ball, pass to the outside of the defense, use hard passes, and practice cross-court passes.

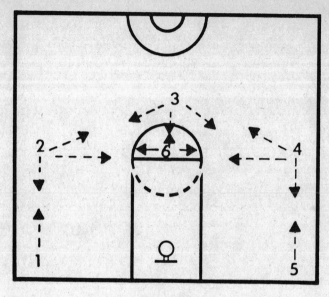

Diagram 9-1

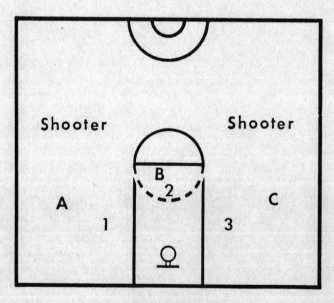

Diagram 9-2

2. Rebounding game. Alternate shots from the two shooters and have A, B, and C go for the rebounds against 1, 2, and 3. The offense can shoot if it gets the ball. The defense clears the ball out to the shooter on the side of the rebound if it gets the ball. You can make it competitive by giving one point for a cleared rebound and two for a made basket. Change every five shots and go to 10 points.

3. Cutting drill. The offense passes and cuts, but must stay on the same half-court as shown by the dotted line. The defense is zone and adjusts to all the cuts,

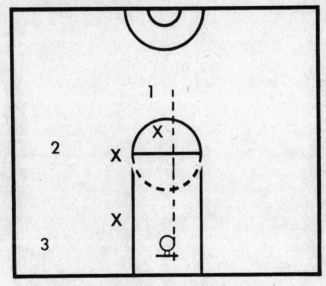

Diagram 9-3

maintaining its basic zone positions. You can add the options of punching and driving to this same drill. Let the offense keep the ball if it can score. Emphasize the points of the give and go, the circle cuts, and the V-cuts. As punching and driving are added, work on the specific execution of those points.

4. Get the ball inside. Players must stay on the same side of the dotted line in diagram 9-4. Post 3 must move

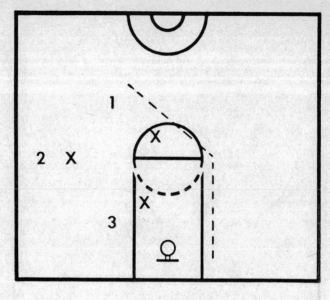

Diagram 9-4

from high to low and vice-versa every third pass. Players 1 and 2 can drive, dribble-pull, or pass the ball inside directly, but their goal is to get the ball inside. They want penetration. You can add a fourth man. Keep ball if you score.

5. Corner-slide drill. This can be worked without defense at first to teach proper cutting and rotation. Then you can allow defense, but the shot must come off one of the cutting moves. The rule in the drill is that anytime the ball is passed to the corner, the man who threw it cuts. See in diagrams 9-5, 9-6 and 9-7 that everytime someone passes to the corner, he cuts to the goal and the other outside players rotate. When working against no defense, use ten passes before a shot is taken. Be sure every third or fourth pass goes to the post, however. And if the post throws to a corner, he cuts to the goal. Against defense, let the scoring team keep the ball.

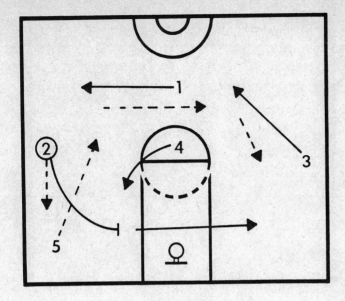

Diagram 9-5

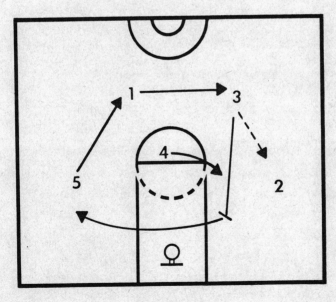

Diagram 9-6

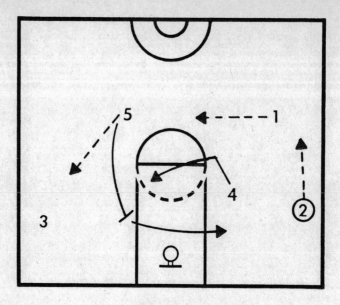

Diagram 9-7

6. Point cut and posts cross drill. The offense lines up
   1-2-2, as shown in 9-8. Point 1 initiates the move with
   a pass to his right and cuts to the corner. On the
   reversal 1 roves the base and 3 passes to 1 and cuts
   just as 1 had done. In diagram 9-10 you see the posts
   cross over as 1 gets the ball and 3 has moved to the
   baseline. The play is continued, with 2 taking his turn
   and doing just what 1 did in 9-8. With no defense the
   play continues for ten passes. The ball must go into
   the posts every third or fourth pass. Against defense
   allow the scoring team to keep the ball. Emphasize
   quick cuts and rotations, creating lanes, sharp passing,
   and staying spread on the offense.

7. High-low post drills.

   a. High-low post passing. Pass the ball around from 1
   to 2 to 3 and back. Everytime the ball goes to 4 he
   turns and 5 crosses under the goal while 2 and 3 move

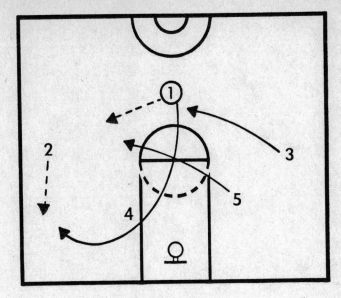

Diagram 9-8

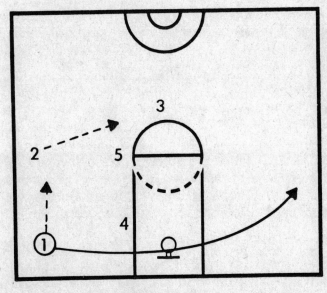

Diagram 9-9

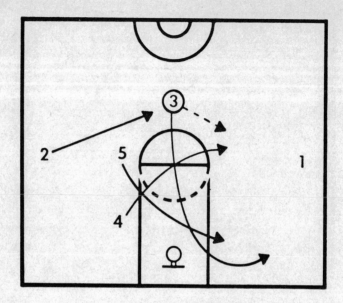

Diagram 9-10

down toward the corner (Diagram 9-11). Posts 4 and 5 change positions every three or four passes. Pass ten times before shooting. Add defense to 4 and 5, and only one of them can shoot.

b. Pop the post drill. The drill is the same as in 7a except 1 uses the dribble-pull move as in diagram 9-12 in order to key the high post to pop out.

c. Drive at the post. Do the same as the drills in 7a and 7b except that 2 or 3 dribble into the lane or corner whenever they want. Posts 4 and 5 pop out a step or two to make room for the drives. On this defense may be added to players 2, 3, 4, and 5.

8. Punch drill. Instruct A, B, and C to play between 1, 2, 3, and 4 so that there is always a gap in front of the offense as in diagram 9-14. Player 1 starts the punch left with 5 and 2 adjusting accordingly. They may shoot if they get a good shot. If not, the drill ends.

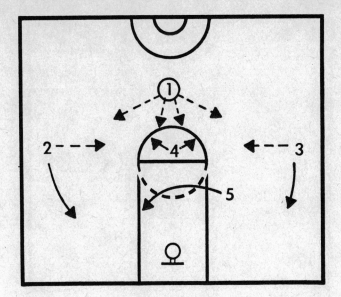

Diagram 9-11

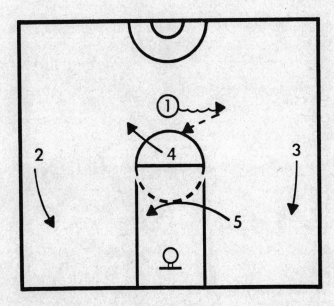

Diagram 9-12

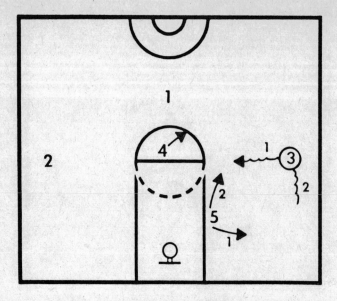

Diagram 9-13

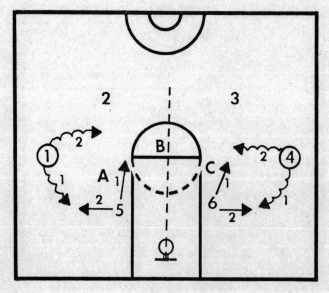

Diagram 9-14

Then, when 1 is finished, 4 makes his move identical to 1 with another ball. After his move 2 punches between A and B. Then it is 3's turn, etc.

9. Dribble-pull and pass drills.

a. Point-high post. Point 1 pulls the defense two bounces to set up his pass to 4. In the diagram he dribbles to his left, but he can dribble either direction, of course. Note 5's cross move. (Diagram 9-15)

Diagram 9-15

b. Wing-post. Wing 3 drives base in 9-16 and inside in 9-17. Post 5 moves according to 3's pull. We like for 3 to clear opposite if he feeds inside in all our low post passing, because it fits into our offense best, but that is optional.

10. The dribble game. The defense plays a four man matching zone against the four man offense. The only way a shot can be taken is through driving. The ball is

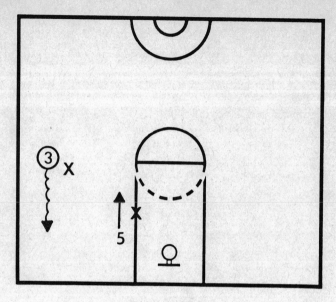

Diagram 9-16

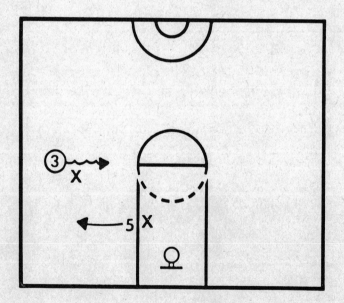

Diagram 9-17

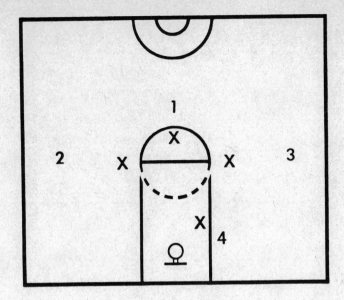

Diagram 9-18

passed until one player can get a good chance to drive one-on-one. The offense keeps the ball as long as it scores. (Diagram 9-18)

11. The cutting game. The same kind of game as in 10 except the players can get shots only off of cuts into the defense. (Diagram 9-19)

12. Post action game. Only the posts may shoot. They go against their men 2-on-2 inside and follow the rules of movement. You can add to the drill by making it 5-on-5, but the only shots can be taken by a post or by a player who is fed directly for the shot by a post man.

13. Screen drills.

    a. Baseline screens. The drill starts with 1 passing to 2 and 4 cuts off of 5 as 5 turns to look back at the ball. 5 will cut off of 3 on the reversal of the ball. Only 3, 4, or 5 may shoot. Keep it if they score. (Diagram 9-21)

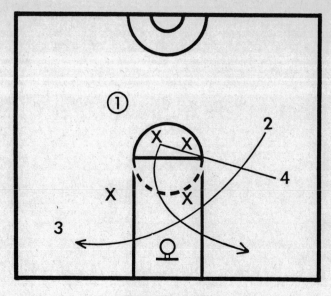

Diagram 9-19

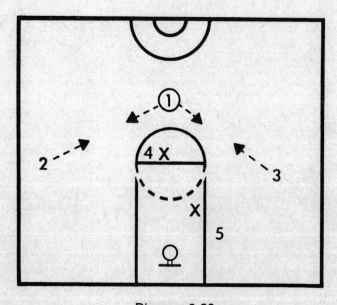

Diagram 9-20

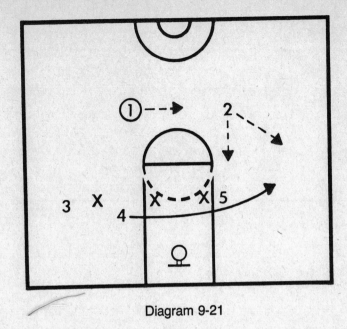

Diagram 9-21

b. Two-man games with wing-point. The manager can throw the ball to 1 as in the diagram 9-22 and 1 and 2 work the two-man game.

c. Two-man games with the base-wing. Same as 13 but with the base and wing screen. (Diagram 9-23)

d. Two-man games with the post-point. Repeat of 13b and c. (Diagram 9-24)

e. You can also have a 5-on-5 game allowing shots to come only as a result of screening tactics just as we have shown games which use cutting, dribble-moves, etc.

14. Teaching the Basic Five moves in general. You can drill the drills separately by selecting any of the many drills shown in this chapter on drills. Soon the team will be able to practice the Basic Five on a 5-on-5 basis. But start allowing this one at a time. That is,

Diagram 9-22

Diagram 9-23

Diagram 9-24

allow only shots which come from one of the specific Basic Five moves at a time. After a few minutes on one of the Basic Five, move on to another. Then, soon you will be able to put the men on a 5-on-5 basis and tell them to use any of the Basic Five as they come up. As the season progresses, the coach can spend maybe a half-hour a week and expect good results in games from the Basic Five. The coach should be sure to mix the defense against the Basic Five in the drills, eventually making changes during practices without telling the offensive players that any change will be made.

INDEX